Solomon Straub

Christian life songs for Sunday school

Solomon Straub

Christian life songs for Sunday school

ISBN/EAN: 9783337264963

Printed in Europe, USA, Canada, Australia, Japan

Cover: Foto ©Lupo / pixelio.de

More available books at **www.hansebooks.com**

PUBLISHED BY
S. W. STRAUB & CO.
CHICAGO.

Copyright, 1890, by S. W. Straub.

SUGGESTIONS.

1. Teach a new piece to the School by having it well sung as a solo or quartet first, so that the beauty of the piece may be recognized by the pupils before they attempt it. Use it once or twice every Sunday until it is properly sung and fixed in the minds of all. Do not merely *try* pieces, but *learn* them *thoroughly*.

2. Insist upon *all* watching the leader, who should conduct with a baton.

3. Explain in simple language the meaning of the words, and insist upon proper expression of them.

4. Do not let the children scream, but keep their voices sweet and pure.

5. Do not sing the same kind of songs in succession. Change the style and character of the pieces as much as possible.

6. Sing one or more solid church tunes at every session. All will like it, and it will make the children feel more at home in the church service to join with the congregation in singing.

7. Remember that the best tunes are not always the easiest, and therefore the more difficult ones should be drilled until they can be sung well. Then *they* will be the favorites.

8. Each family should be supplied with books, so that the songs may be learned and used in the home.

9. The "Opening Services" will be found very pleasant and useful. They may be changed, or parts omitted. The Chant may be omitted, and an extemporaneous prayer may take the place of the printed prayer.

10. Use "Christian Life Songs" not only in the Sunday School, but in the regular Prayer Meeting, Young People's Meeting, and frequently in the Congregation, to the end that the power of sacred music may strengthen the bond of union among all, and lift them to higher planes of "Christian Life."

S. W. STRAUB.

CHRISTIAN LIFE SONGS.

PRAISE AND THANKSGIVING.

1   Be Joyful in God.

MONTGOMERY.   S. W. STRAUB.

1. Be joy - ful in God, all ye lands of the earth, Oh,
2. Je - ho - vah is God, and Je - ho - vah a - lone, Cre-
3. Oh, en - ter his gates with thanks-giv - ing and song; Your
4. For good is the Lord, in - ex - pres - si - bly good, And

serve him with glad - ness and fear; Ex - ult in his pres - ence with
a - tor and rul - er o'er all; And we are his peo - ple, his
vows in his tem - ple pro - claim: His praise with me - lo - dious ac-
we are the work of his hand; His mer - cy and truth from e-

mu - sic and mirth; With love and de - vo - tion draw near.
scep - tre we own; His sheep, and we fol - low his call.
cord - ance pro - long, And bless his a - do - ra - ble name.
ter - ni - ty stood, And shall to e - ter - ni - ty stand.

PRAISE AND THANKSGIVING.

3 Sweet is the Work, my God, my King.
ISAAC WATTS. Arr. fr. SCHUMANN.

1. Sweet is the work, my God, my King! To praise thy name, give thanks, and sing;
2. Sweet is the day of sa-cred rest; No mor-tal cares shall seize my breast
3. My heart shall tri-umph in my Lord, And bless his works, and bless his word;

To show thy love by morn-ing light, and talk of all thy truth at night.
Oh! may my heart in tune be found, Like Da-vid's harp of sol-emn sound!
Thy words of grace, how bright they shine! How deep thy coun-sels! how di-vine!

4 Help Us to Praise.

1. Come, thou Al-might-y King, Help us thy name to sing, Help us to praise; Fa-ther all
2. Come, thou all gracious Lord! By heav'n and earth adored. Our prayer attend! Come, and thy
3. Nev-er from us de-part; Rule thou in ev-'ry heart, Hence, evermore! Thy sovereign

glo-ri-ous, O'er all vic-to-ri-ous, Come, and reign o-ver us, Ancient of days!
chil-dren bless; Give thy good word success; Make thine own holiness On us de-scend
maj-es-ty May we in glo-ry see, And to e-ter-ni-ty Love and a-dore!

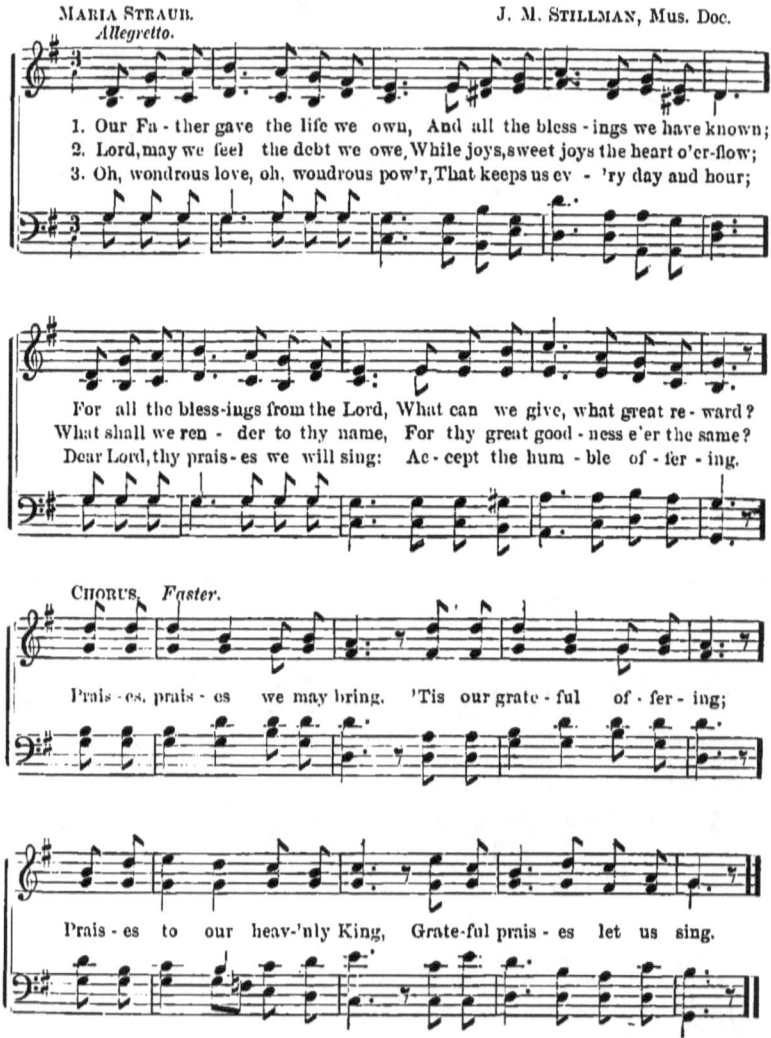

PRAISE AND THANKSGIVING.

6 Sabbath Morning.

REV. GEO. SCHOBR. S. W. STRAUB.
Rather fast.

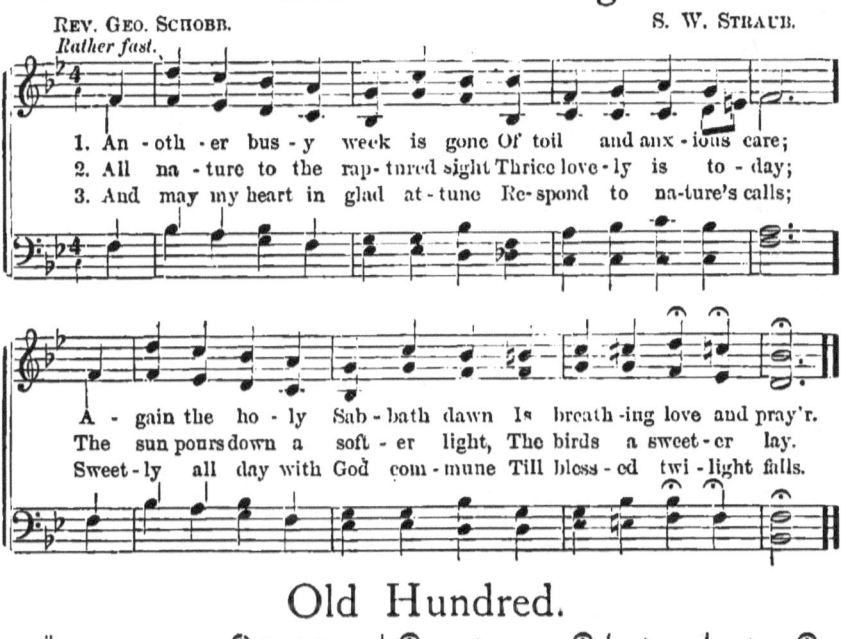

1. An-oth-er bus-y week is gone Of toil and anx-ious care;
   A-gain the ho-ly Sab-bath dawn Is breath-ing love and pray'r.
2. All na-ture to the rap-tured sight Thrice love-ly is to-day;
   The sun pours down a soft-er light, The birds a sweet-er lay.
3. And may my heart in glad at-tune Re-spond to na-ture's calls;
   Sweet-ly all day with God com-mune Till bless-ed twi-light falls.

Old Hundred.

7
1. Be thou, O God, exalted high;
   And as thy glory fills the sky,
   So let it be on earth displayed,
   Till thou art here, as there, obeyed.

2. O God, our hearts are fixed and bent
   Their thankful tribute to present;
   And, with the heart, the voice we'll raise
   To thee, our God, in songs of praise.

3. Thy praises, Lord, we will resound
   To all the listening nations round;
   Thy mercy highest heaven transcends;
   Thy truth beyond the clouds extends.

8
1. Oh, render thanks to God above,
   The fountain of eternal love,
   Whose mercy firm, through ages past
   Hath stood, and shall forever last.

2. Who can his mighty deeds express,
   Not only vast, but numberless?
   What mortal eloquence can raise
   His tribute of immortal praise?

3. Extend to me that favor, Lord,
   Thou to thy chosen dost afford:
   When thou return'st to set them free,
   Let thy salvation visit me.

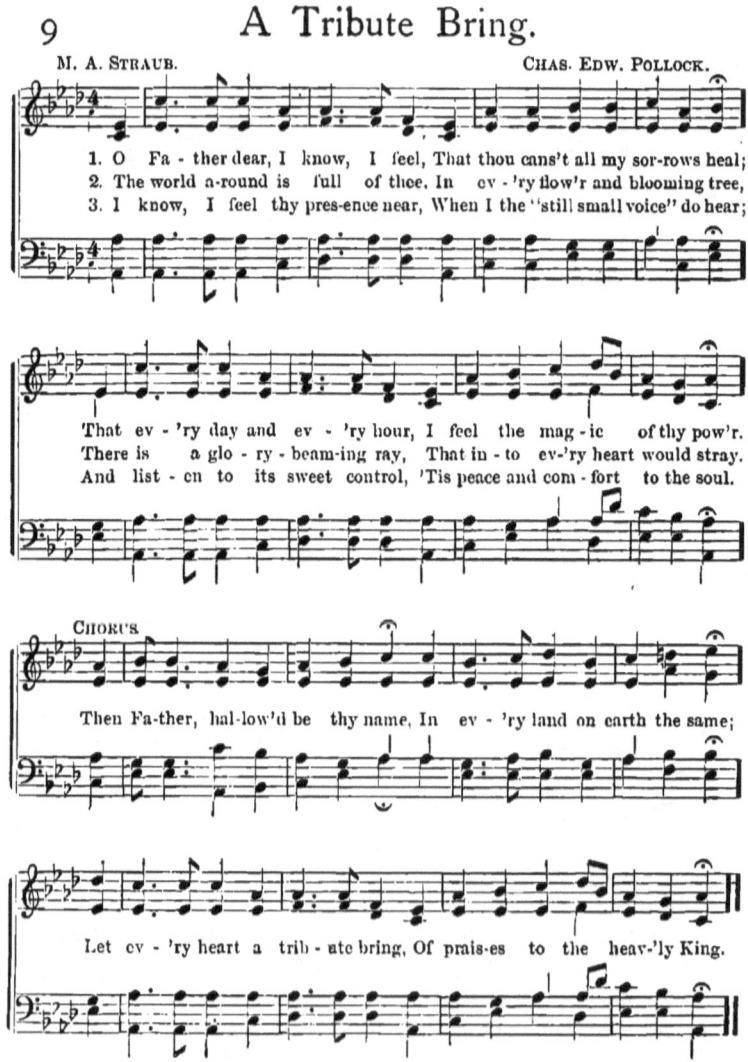

PRAISE AND THANKSGIVING.

10. Thanksgiving Hymn.

Rev. J. M. RUTHRAUFF. T. MARTIN TOWNE.

1. Lord God of ho - li - ness, Source of all bless - ed - ness, Di - rect our ways; O may Thy mer - cy flow, Thro' all the earth be - low, And ev - 'ry good be - stow, Thro' all our days.
2. Thou dost all na - tions prove, By Thy blest word they move. Thy word and love; O shed Thy ho - ly light, A - round our path - way bright, And lead us ev - er right, O Lord a - bove.
3. All foun - tains from Thee flow, The sun - beams dost be - stow, The in - crease give; Then may our land be blest, With Thy rich boun - ties' best, And with Thy heav'n - ly rest, In whom we live.
4. Now may our hearts re - joice, And with u - nit - ed voice, Thy prais - es sing; O may sweet an - thems ring, From all the na - tions spring, To Thee all glo - ry bring, Je - ho - vah King.

11. Nettleton or Greenville.

Key of E♭.

1. Come, thou Fount of every blessing
Tune my heart to sing thy grace
Streams of mercy, never ceasing,
Call for songs of loudest praise,
Praise the mount—I'm fixed upon it—
Mount of thy redeeming love,
Teach me some melodious sonnet,
Sung by flaming tongues above;

Key of F.

2. O, to grace how great a debtor,
Daily I'm constrained to be!
Let thy goodness, like a fetter,
Bind my wandering heart to thee,
Prone to wander, Lord, I feel it;
Prone to leave the God I love;
Here's my heart, O, take and seal it,
Seal it for thy courts above.

PRAISE AND THANKSGIVING.

We May not Forget—Concluded.

Ne'er for-get the might-y love Of our Fa-ther dear a-bove.

15 Praise to Thee.

MARY E. C. WYETH.　　　　　　　　　　S. W. S. Chorus, arr.

Duet.

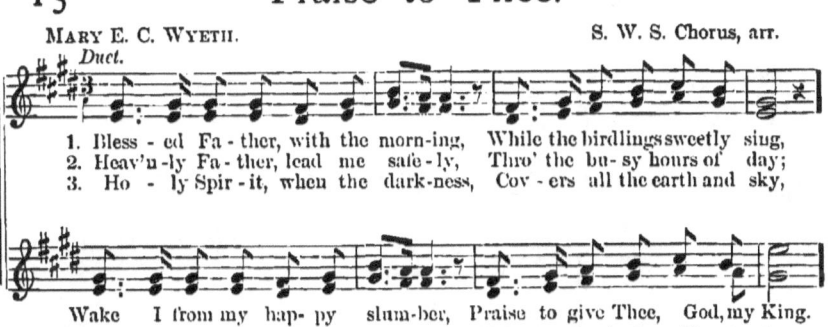

1. Bless-ed Fa-ther, with the morn-ing, While the birdlings sweetly sing,
2. Heav'n-ly Fa-ther, lead me safe-ly, Thro' the bu-sy hours of day;
3. Ho-ly Spir-it, when the dark-ness, Cov-ers all the earth and sky,

Wake I from my hap-py slum-ber, Praise to give Thee, God, my King.
Keep my heed-less feet from stray-ing, Help me, Lord, thy will t'o-bey.
Let no guilt-y con science haunt me, As up-on my couch I lie.

CHORUS. *Louder and faster.*

Praise to thee, O God my King, Praise to thee I'll ev-er sing,

For the mag-ic of thy love, Sent to me from heav'n a-bove.

PRAISE AND THANKSGIVING.

16 We're Children of a King.

Mrs. ADALINE H. BEERY. T. MARTIN TOWNE.
Cheerfully.

1. We're a band of hap-py chil-dren, In a world of sin and care;
2. When we're sad he folds us to him; And when wea-ry, gives us rest;
3. We are weak to do him ser-vice, But his arm is won-drous strong;

In our dai-ly walks and la-bors God's dear love and grace we share.
When we go a-stray he seeks us, Brings us to his King-dom blest.
He's our Fa-ther, Friend and Shep-herd, and we wor-ship him with song.

CHORUS.

Come and join our glad ho-san-nas, Let the air with mu-sic ring!

We are heirs to glo-rious treas-ure, For we're chil-dren of a King.

17. Public Worship.

Joyously.   Arr. by S. W. STRAUB.

1. How pleas-ant, how di-vine-ly fair, O Lord of Hosts, thy dwell-ings are!
2. Blest are the souls that find a place With-in the tem-ple of thy grace;
3. Blest are the men whose hearts are set To find the way to Zi-on's gate;
4. Cheer-ful they walk with growing strength, Till all shall meet in heav'n at length;

With long de-sire my spir-it faints To meet th'as-sem-blies of thy saints.
Where they be-hold thy gent-ler rays, And seek thy face and learn thy praise.
God is their strength; and thro' the road They lean up-on their help-er, God.
Till all be-fore thy face ap-pear, And join in no-bler wor-ship there

18. Evening Song.

Earnestly.   J. BARNBY.

1. Great God! to thee my even-ing song With hum-ble grat-i-tude I raise;
2. My days, un-cloud-ed as they pass, And ev-'ry gen-tly roll-ing hour,
3. Let this blest hope mine eye-lids close; With sleep re-fresh my fee-ble frame;

Oh, let thy mer-cy tune my tongue, And fill my heart with live-ly praise.
Are mon-u-ments of wondrous grace, And wit-ness to thy love and pow'r.
Safe in thy care may I re-pose, And wake with prais-es to thy name.

PRAISE AND THANKSGIVING.

19. I'll Remember my Creator.

"Remember now thy Creator, in the days of thy youth." Eccl. xii: 1.

MARIA STRAUB.   S. W. STRAUB.

1. I'll re-mem-ber my Cre-a-tor, In the sun-ny days of youth;
2. In the morn-ing when I wak-en From the slumbers of the night,
3. I should love and serve him ev-er, Who has giv-en life and friends;

I'll re-mem-ber him the Giv-er, And will learn his pre-cious truth.
I will not for-get to praise Him, Who a-gain has bro't the light.
I'll re-mem-ber my Cre-a-tor, For the blessings that he sends.

CHORUS.

I'll re-mem-ber, remember, Re-mem-ber my Cre-a-tor in the days of my youth,

rit.

Re-mem-ber, re-mem-ber, Re-mem-ber, my Cre-a-tor in the days of my youth.

PRAISE AND THANKSGIVING.

21. Praise the Lord!

BEETHOVEN.

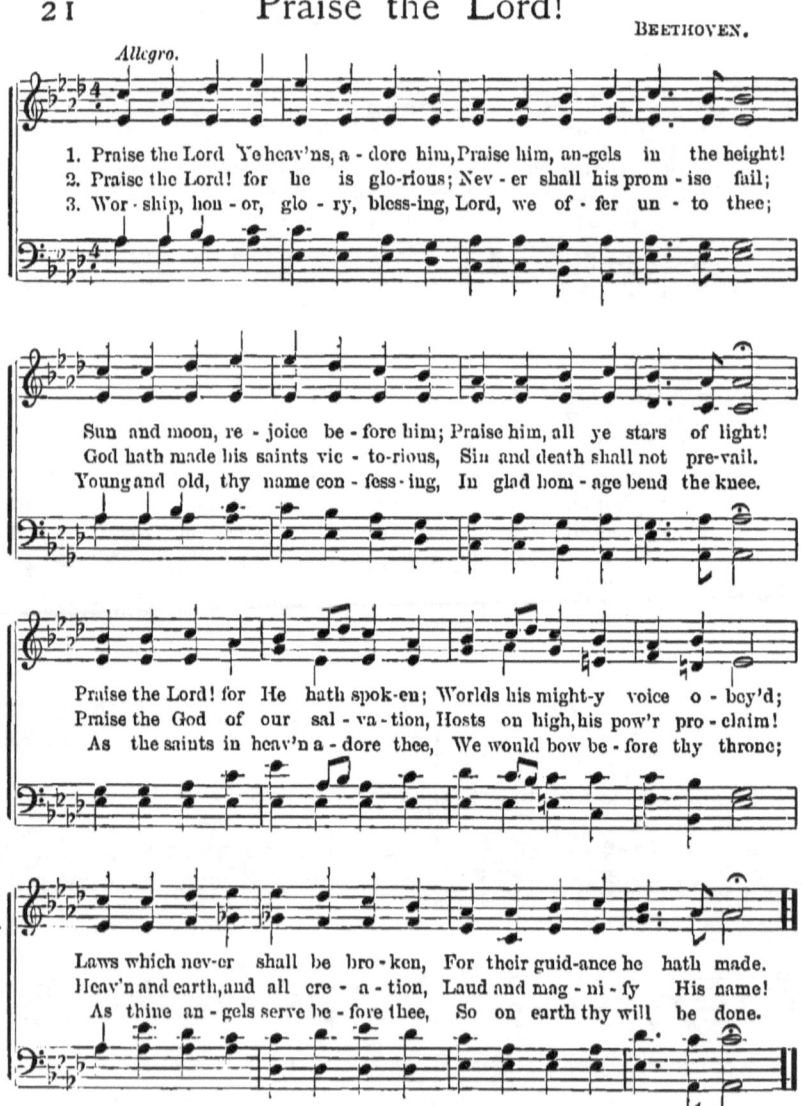

1. Praise the Lord! Ye heav'ns, a - dore him, Praise him, an-gels in the height!
2. Praise the Lord! for he is glo-rious; Nev - er shall his prom - ise fail;
3. Wor - ship, hon - or, glo - ry, bless-ing, Lord, we of - fer un - to thee;

Sun and moon, re - joice be - fore him; Praise him, all ye stars of light!
God hath made his saints vic - to-rious, Sin and death shall not pre-vail.
Young and old, thy name con - fess-ing, In glad hom - age bend the knee.

Praise the Lord! for He hath spok-en; Worlds his might-y voice o - bey'd;
Praise the God of our sal - va-tion, Hosts on high, his pow'r pro - claim!
As the saints in heav'n a - dore thee, We would bow be - fore thy throne;

Laws which nev-er shall be bro-ken, For their guid-ance he hath made.
Heav'n and earth, and all cre - a - tion, Laud and mag - ni - fy His name!
As thine an - gels serve be - fore thee, So on earth thy will be done.

PRAISE AND THANKSGIVING.

22 Morning Hymn.

From the German by MARIA STRAUB.   Arr. by S. W. S.

1. O my Fa-ther, thee I thank For the bless-ings of the night.
2. All I do and think this day, Let it be in love for thee;
3. I would be so good and true, That when night-ly I'm a-sleep,

With thy love, I am en-twined, Thou hast sent an an-gel kind,
Thro' the ma-zes that I meet, Fa-ther guide my wand'-ing feet,
My kind an-gel from the skies O'er me e'er will beam his eyes,

An-gel kind, an an-gel bright, To guard me thro' the night.
And a grate-ful heart give me For bless-ings all from thee.
And me in my slum-bers keep, Safe-ly and sweet-ly keep.

23

AUTUMN. Key of A Flat.

1. God is in his holy temple:
   Thoughts of earth, be silent now,
   While with reverence we assemble,
   And before his presence bow!
   He is with us now and ever,
   When we call upon his name,
   Aiding every good endeavor,
   Guiding every upward aim.

2. God is in his holy temple:—
   In the pure and holy mind;
   In the reverent heart and simple:
   In the soul from sense refined:
   Then let every low emotion,
   Banished far and silent be!
   And our souls, in pure devotion,
   Lord, be temples worthy thee!

24 Welcome to Our Sabbath Home.

Cheerfully. — FRANK M. DAVIS.

1. Joy-ful hearts and smil-ing fac - es Gath - er in our school to - day;
2. Gently lead our hearts, O Sav - ior! Help us, lest we go a - stray;
3. May the grace of God the Fa - ther, And the Sav-ior's ten - der love,

Lov-ing words and gen - tle mu - sic Min - gle in our o - p'ning lay.
Teach us al- ways to o - bey Thee, Guide us in the nar - row way.
With the bless-ed Spir - it's fa - vor, Rest up - on us from a - bove.

CHORUS.

O lis - ten to the hap-py song of greet - ing, Sweetly sounding 'neath the dome,
While in Je-sus' name we bid thee wel - come, Wel-come to our Sab-bath home.

PRAISE AND THANKSGIVING.

25. I Love the Giver More.

M. S.
Brightly.
S. W. S.

1. I love to see the beau-teous flowers, To view them o'er and o'er;
2. I love the birds, dear lit-tle birds, That charm me with their glee;
3. I love the beau-ti-ful and good, They bring me pleas-ure true;

I love the cheer-y lit-tle things, But love the Giv-er more.
'Tis God who sends the song-bird here, To war-ble sweet to me.
I love thy bless-ings O my Lord, I can but love thee too.

CHORUS.

I love him more, I love him more, I love the Giv-er more;

I love life's bless-ings, but I love My God, the Giv-er, more.

PRAISE AND THANKSGIVING.

26 God of My Life.

S. W. STRAUB.

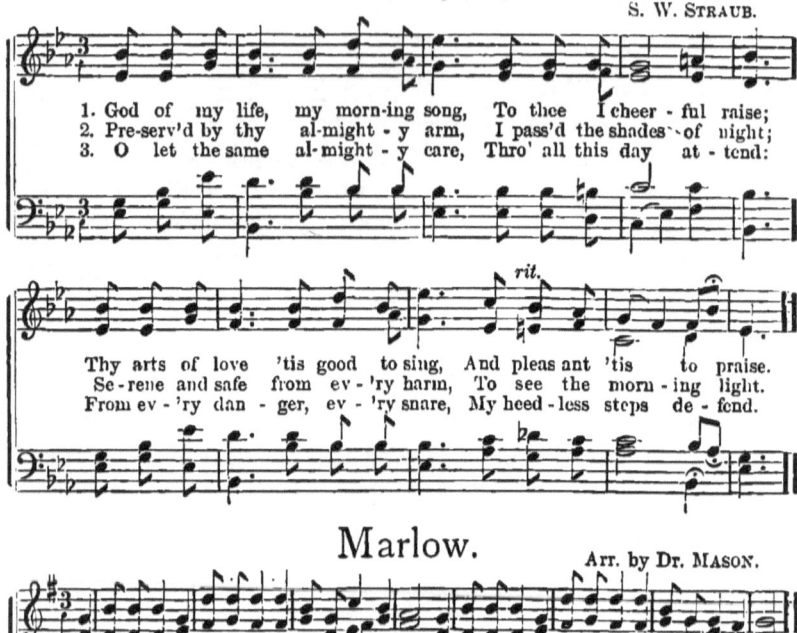

1. God of my life, my morning song, To thee I cheerful raise;
2. Preserv'd by thy almighty arm, I pass'd the shades of night;
3. O let the same almighty care, Thro' all this day attend:

Thy arts of love 'tis good to sing, And pleasant 'tis to praise.
Serene and safe from ev'ry harm, To see the morning light.
From ev'ry danger, ev'ry snare, My heedless steps defend.

Marlow.

Arr. by Dr. MASON.

27

1. Hail! Source of light, of life and love,
And joys that never end;
In whom all creatures live and move;
Creator, Father, Friend.

2. All space is with thy presence crowned;
Creation owns thy care;
Each spot in nature's ample round,
Proclaims that God is there.

3. Attuned to praise be every voice;
Let not one heart be sad;
Jehovah reigns! Let earth rejoice;
Let all the isle be glad.

4. Then sound the anthem loud and long
In sweetest, loftiest strains;
And be the burden of the song,
The Lord, Jehovah, reigns!

28

1. Eternal Wisdom, thee we praise;
Thee all thy creatures sing; [seas.
While with thy name, rocks, hills and
And heaven's high palace, ring.

2. Thy hand, how wide it spreads the sky!
How glorious to behold!
Tinged with a blue of heavenly dye,
And decked with sparkling gold.

3. Thy glories blaze all nature round,
And strike the gazing sight,
Thro' skies, and seas, and solid ground,
With terror and delight.

PRAYER AND ASPIRATION.

30 Out of the Depths.

EVANGELINE.   S. W. STRAUB.

1. O Fa-ther, hear my plead-ing pray'rs, And help thy help-less one;
   The way is dark and full of snares, And I am all a-lone.
   I can not see—but let me know Thy hand doth lead me on;
   I can-not see—but let me know Thy hand doth lead me on.

2. My soul shrinks back with fears be-set, And ter-rors all un-tried,
   Rise up to meet me as I go; Be thou my guard and guide;
   I shall be safe if thou wilt stay For-ev-er at my side;
   I shall be safe if thou wilt stay For-ev-er at my side.

3. If I should mur-mur that my life Is dark, and drear, and chill,
   O chide me with thy gen-tle voice And whis-per, "Peace! be still!"
   Nor let my spir-it long for rest Till I have done thy will,
   Nor let my spir-it long for rest Till I have done thy will.

PRAISE AND ASPARATION.

33 Abide with me!

H. F. LYTE.
W. H. MONK.
With expression.

1. A - bide with me! fast falls the e - ven - tide; The dark - ness
deep - ens; Lord, with me a - bide! When oth - er help - ers
fail, and com - forts flee, Help of the help-less, O a - bide with me!

2. Swift to its close ebbs out life's lit - tle day; Earth's joys' grow
dim, its glo - ries pass a - way; Change and de - cay in
all a - round I see; O Thou, who chang-est not, a - bide with me!

3. I need thy pres - ence ev - 'ry pass-ing hour; What but Thy
grace can foil the tempt - er's pow'r? Who like Thy - self my
guide and stay can be? Thro' cloud and sun-shine, O a - bide with me!

4. Hold Thou Thy cross be - fore my clos - ing eyes; Shine thro' the
gloom, and point me to the skies. Heav'n's morn - ing breaks, and
earth's vain shad-ows flee! In life, in death, O Lord, a - bide with me!

'34 Bethany.
Key of G.

1. Nearer, my God to thee,
   Nearer to thee!
   E'en though it be a cross
   That raiseth me,
   Still all my song shall be,
   Nearer, my God, to thee!
   Nearer to thee!

2. Though like a wanderer,
   The sun gone down,
   Darkness comes over me,
   My rest a stone;
   Yet in my dreams I'd be
   Nearer, my God, to thee,
   Nearer to thee!

3. There let my way appear
   Steps unto heaven;
   All that thou sendest me
   In mercy given;
   Angles to beckon me
   Nearer, my God, to thee,
   Nearer to thee!

PRAYER AND ASPIRATION.

35 Thy Kingdom Come.

MARIA STRAUB. S. W. STRAUB.
Andante.

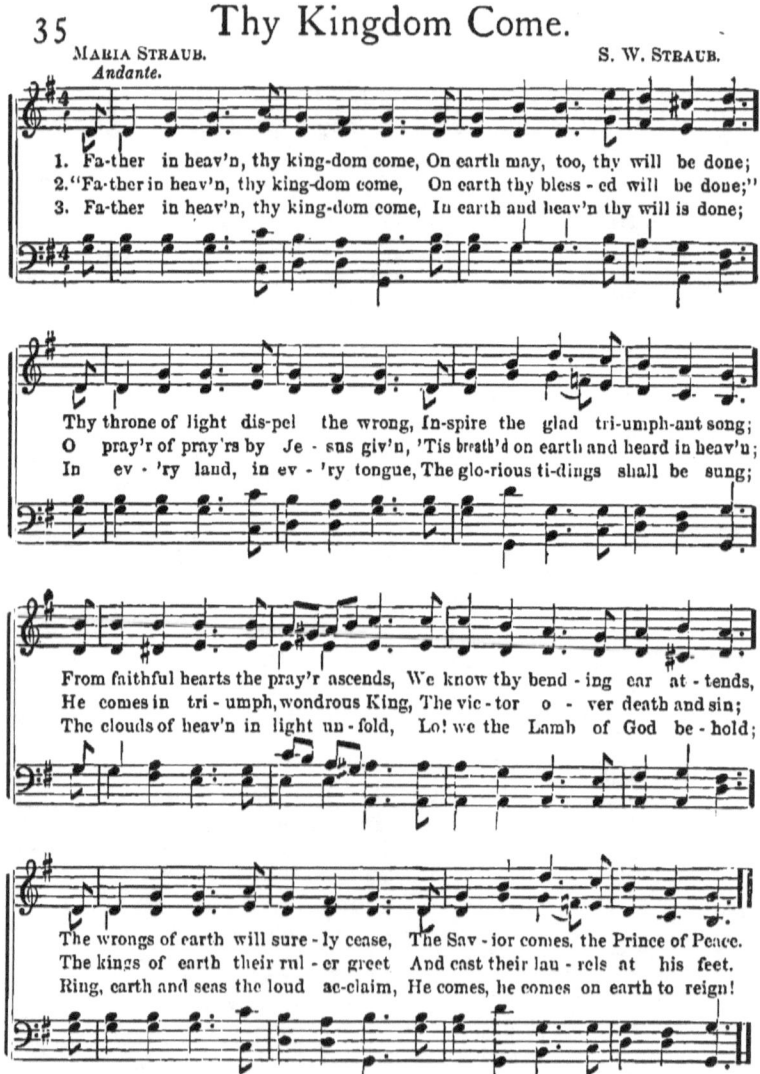

1. Fa-ther in heav'n, thy king-dom come, On earth may, too, thy will be done;
2. "Fa-ther in heav'n, thy king-dom come, On earth thy bless-ed will be done;"
3. Fa-ther in heav'n, thy king-dom come, In earth and heav'n thy will is done;

Thy throne of light dis-pel the wrong, In-spire the glad tri-umph-ant song;
O pray'r of pray'rs by Je-sus giv'n, 'Tis breath'd on earth and heard in heav'n;
In ev-'ry land, in ev-'ry tongue, The glo-rious ti-dings shall be sung;

From faithful hearts the pray'r ascends, We know thy bend-ing ear at-tends,
He comes in tri-umph, wondrous King, The vic-tor o-ver death and sin;
The clouds of heav'n in light un-fold, Lo! we the Lamb of God be-hold;

The wrongs of earth will sure-ly cease, The Sav-ior comes, the Prince of Peace.
The kings of earth their rul-er greet And cast their lau-rels at his feet.
Ring, earth and seas the loud ac-claim, He comes, he comes on earth to reign!

PRAYER AND ASPIRATION.

36 Nearer I'd Be.

THOS. MACKELLAR.   S. W. STRAUB.

Fervently.

1. Near - er to thy heart of love, Near - er to thy hand of pow'r:
2. Near - er when the morn shall break, Near - er when the sun goes down,
3. Near - er, Je - sus, to thy breast, As my dai - ly need is more.

Je - sus, near - er ev - 'ry hour, Lift me to the life a - bove.
Let thy lov - ing kind - ness crown, All the way my feet should take.
Till thou o - pen - est the door Lead - ing to the heav'n - ly rest.

CHORUS.

Near - er, near - er, near - er I'd be,
Near - er I'd be, near - er I'd be, Near - er, yes, near - er I'd be,

Last time repeat pp.

Near - er near - er, near - er to thee.
Near - er to thee, near - er to thee, Near - er, oh, near - er to thee.

PRAYER AND ASPIRATION.

Savior, Walk With Me.—Concluded.

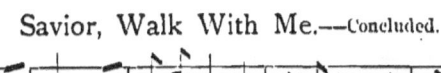

path be thine and mine; I need thee, need thee more and more O take my hand in thine.

38 Upward.

Arr. from BEETHOVEN.

1. Up-ward, Fa-ther, turn our eyes, Up-ward let our spir-its rise;
2. Up-ward reach-ing, while we pray, In thine hand our hearts to lay;
3. Up-ward may we learn to strive In the life we dai-ly live.

From the things that keep from Thee   Set us now at lib-er-ty!
Let us find what most we need—   One to com-fort. strengthen, lead,
Mov'd by long-ing thus to   be   Draw-ing near-er un-to Thee!

39 Greenville.
Key of F.

1. Far from mortal cares retreating,
Sordid hopes, and vain desires;
Here our willing footsteps meeting,
Every heart to heaven aspires.

2. From the fount of glory beaming,
Light celestial cheers our eyes;
Mercy from above proclaiming
Peace and pardon from the skies.

3. Who may share this great salvation?
Every pure and humble mind,
Every kindred, tongue and nation,
From the stains of guilt refined.

4. Blessings all around bestowing,
God withholds his care from none,
Grace and mercy ever flowing
From the fountain of his throne.

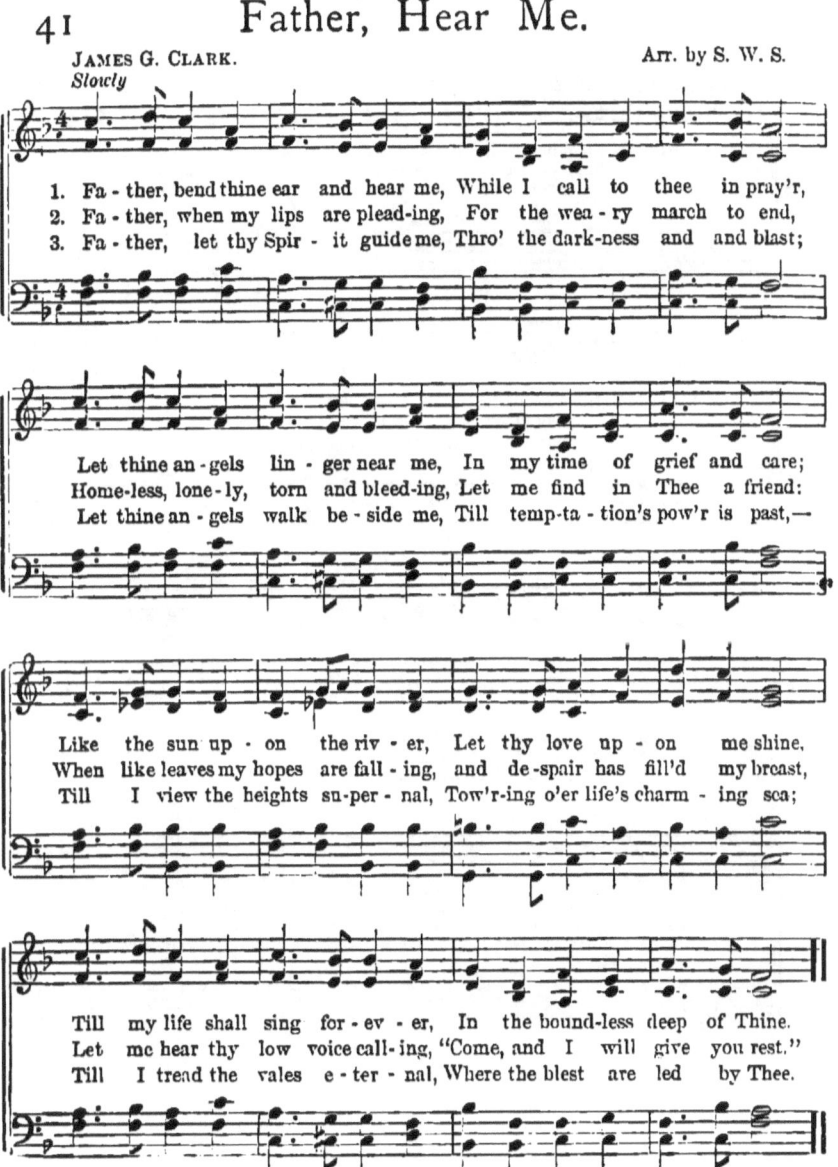

PRAYER AND ASPIRATION.

43. Prayer for Purity.

GEO. SCHOBB.   S. W. S.

1. Oh! that I were pure in heart, Washed and white as snow with-in;
Pure and ho-ly as thou art, Free from ev-'ry stain of sin,
But ab-hor-ing what is base, Fired with zeal that fal-ters not.

2. Je-sus, soul of pu-ri-ty, Thou whose life was all di-vine,
Ev-er live and rule in me, Mould-ing all my life to thine;
So shall I be pure in heart, Washed and white as snow with-in.
Pure and ho-ly as thou art, Free from ev-'ry stain of sin.

Pray on, My Brother.—Concluded.

trust my guid-ing hand, I will safe-ly lead you to the bet-ter land."

45. Savior, be ever Near.

MARIA STRAUB.   S. W. STRAUB.

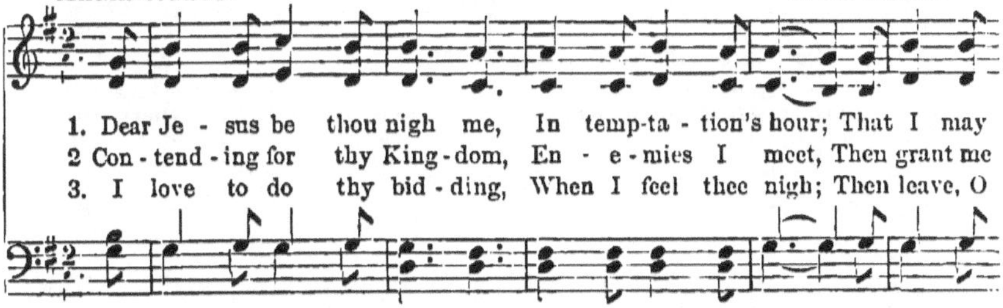

1. Dear Je-sus be thou nigh me, In temp-ta-tion's hour; That I may ne'er de-ny thee, Give re-strain-ing pow'r.
2. Con-tend-ing for thy King-dom, En-e-mies I meet, Then grant me strength and wis-dom, That I may de-feat.
3. I love to do thy bid-ding, When I feel thee nigh; Then leave, O leave me nev-er, Hear my hum-ble cry.

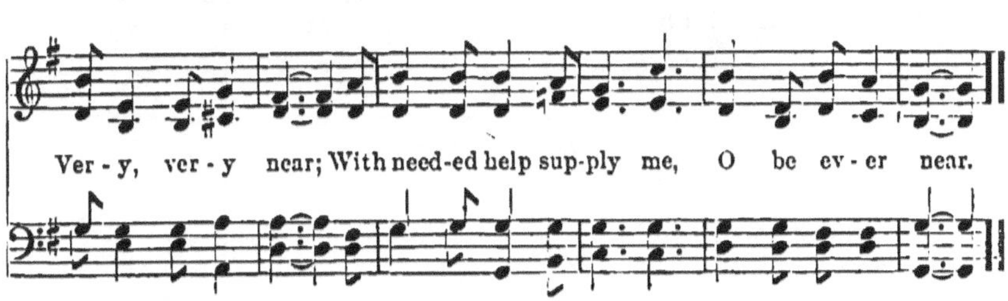

CHORUS.

Sav-ior, be thou nigh me, Ver-y, ver-y near; With need-ed help sup-ply me, O be ev-er near.

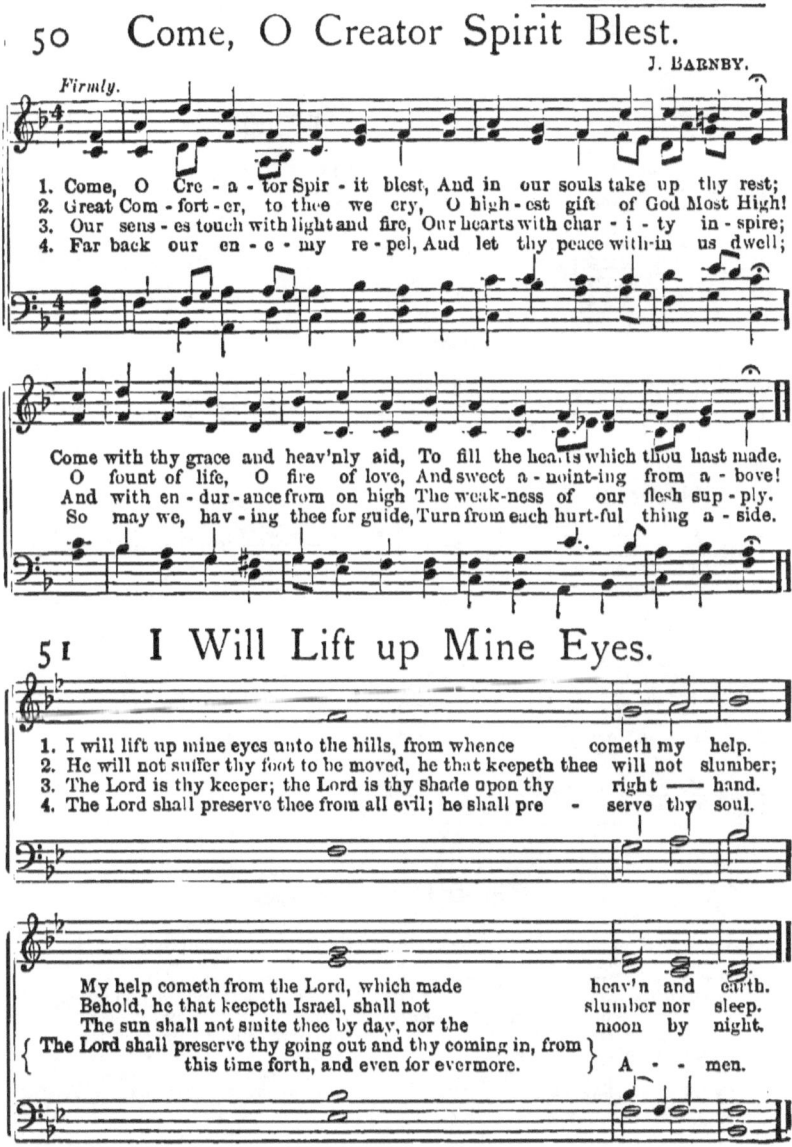

PRAYER AND ASPIRATION.

52. Savior, Bless the Little Ones.

M. S.   S. W. S.

1. Savior, bless a lit-tle child, Make me happy now; Let me feel thy lov-ing hand
2. Lord, I know thou lovest me, Then draw very near; I would feel thee by my side,
3. Savior, make us lov-ing too, Tender, good and kind; When our footsteps go astray,

CHORUS.

On my ten-der brow.   Sav-ior, bless the lit-tle ones, As of old, as of old;
Know that thou art near.
Help the way to find.

Take us in thy lov-ing arms, As thou didst the child-ren of old.

53. Sweet Hour of Prayer.
Key of D.

1 Sweet hour of prayer, sweet hour of prayer,
That calls me from a world of care,
And bids me at my Father's throne
Make all my wants and wishes known;
In seasons of distress and grief,
My soul has often found relief,
||:And oft escaped the tempter's snare,
By thy return, sweet hour of prayer.:||

2 Sweet hour of prayer, sweet hour of prayer,
Thy wings shall my petition bear
To him whose truth and faithfulness
Engage the waiting soul to bless;
And since he bids me seek his face,
Believe his word, and trust his grace,
||:I'll cast on him my every care,
And wait for thee sweet hour of prayer.:||

PRAYER AND ASPIRATION.

54 Descend Upon Us.

Rev. JOEL SWARTZ, D. D. S. W. STRAUB.

1. Spir-it of life and truth and love, Our Com-fort-er and Guide,
2. Shine Thou up-on the writ-ten word, And on our vis-ion shine,
3. And guide us in the paths of peace Thro' life's un-e-ven way,

De-scend up-on us, Heavenly Dove. And with our souls a-bide!
That we may see our Sav-ior, Lord, In ev-'ry grac-ious line.
Un-til these earth-ly wand-rings cease In heav-en's un-clouded day.

55 Prayer for Forgiveness.

Anon.

1. Now let our prayers ascend to thee, Thou great and ho-ly One;
2. Oh, let us feel how frail we are, How much we need thy grace;
3. Our sins, a-las! be-fore thee rise; Thou knowest all our guilt:
4. For-give our sins, thy Spir-it grant, Let love our souls re-fine,

A-bove the world raise thou our hearts, In us thy will be done.
Oh, strengthen, Lord, our faint-ing souls, While here we seek thy face!
Let not our faith, our hope, our trust, On earth-ly things be built.
And heavenly peace and ho-ly hope As-sure that we are thine.

59. Unfailing Love.

EBEN E. REXFORD. (Better as Solo and Chorus.) S. W. STRAUB.

GOD'S LOVE.

1. I read the dear old prom-ise In times when wea-ry grown, Of love that nev-er fail-eth To seek and find its own. Sweet are the words with com-fort As thro' the land I go, That love has failed none ev-er, And can-not fail, we know.

2. No mat-ter what be-tides us, Here in the low-er land, We turn from cares that try us To reach a help-ing hand. We lean on love un-fail-ing, An arm that's strong and true, And feel it sure and stead-fast The whole long jour-ney through.

3. O love so like a fount-ain The sum-mers can-not dry, You fall on hearts grown wea-ry Like sweet rain from the sky. Thy gentle show'rs re-fresh us, And trust-ful-ly we say, The love that failed none ev-er Will fol-low all the way.

CHORUS.

O, sweet the words with com-fort To

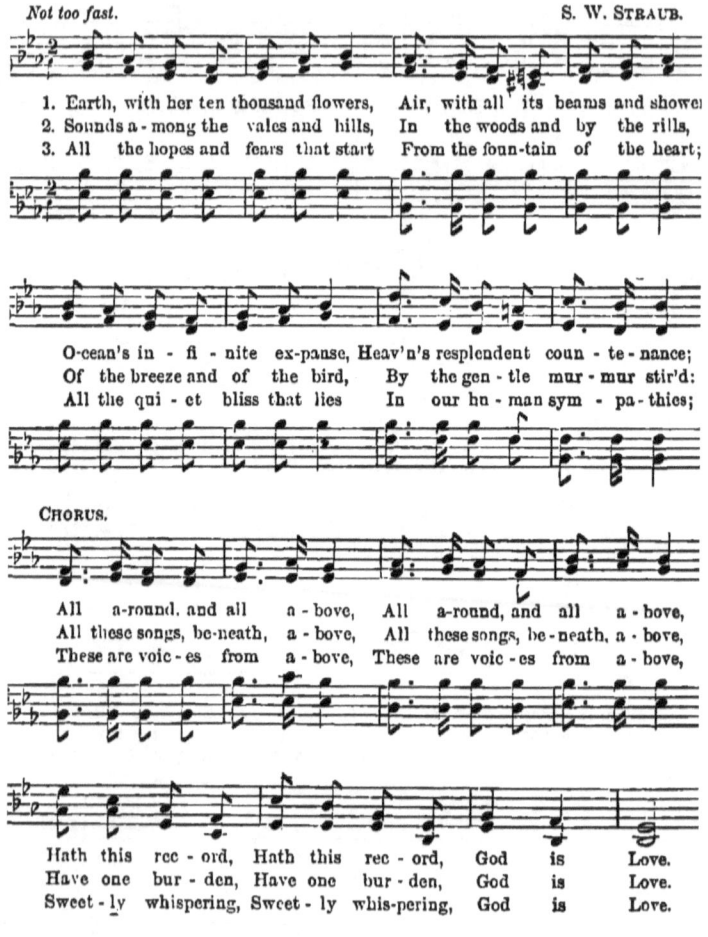

GOD'S LOVE.

62 God's All-Embracing Love.

1. Thou Grace di-vine, en-cir-cling all! A sound-less, shore-less sea;
2. When o-ver diz-zy steeps we go, One soft hand blinds our eyes;
3. And tho' we turn as from thy face, And wan-der wide and long,
4. But not a-lone thy care we claim, Our way-ward steps to win;
5. And filled and quickened by thy breath, Our souls are strong and free

Where-in at last our souls shall fall; O love of God most free.
The oth-er leads us safe and slow, O love of God most wise!
Thou hold'st us still in thine em-brace, O love of God most strong!
We know thee by a dear-er name, O love of God with - in!
To rise o'er sin, and fear, and death, O love of God, to thee!

Stockwell.   D. E. JONES.

63

1 Hail, the God of our salvation,
  Triumph in redeeming love!
  Let us all, with exultation,
  Imitate the blest above.

2 Light of those whose dreary dwelling
  Bordered on the shades of death,
  He hath, by his grace revealing,
  Scattered all the clouds beneath.

3 Father, source of all compassion,
  Pure, unbounded love thou art;
  Hail the God of our salvation,
  Praise him, every thankful heart!

64

1 God is love; his mercy brightens
  All the path in which we rove;
  Bliss he wakes, and woe he lightens;
  God is wisdom, God is love.

2 Chance and change are busy ever;
  Man decays, and ages move;
  But his mercy waneth never:
  God is wisdom, God is love.

3 He with earthly care entwineth
  Hope and comfort from above;
  Everywhere his glory shineth:
  God is wisdom, God is love.

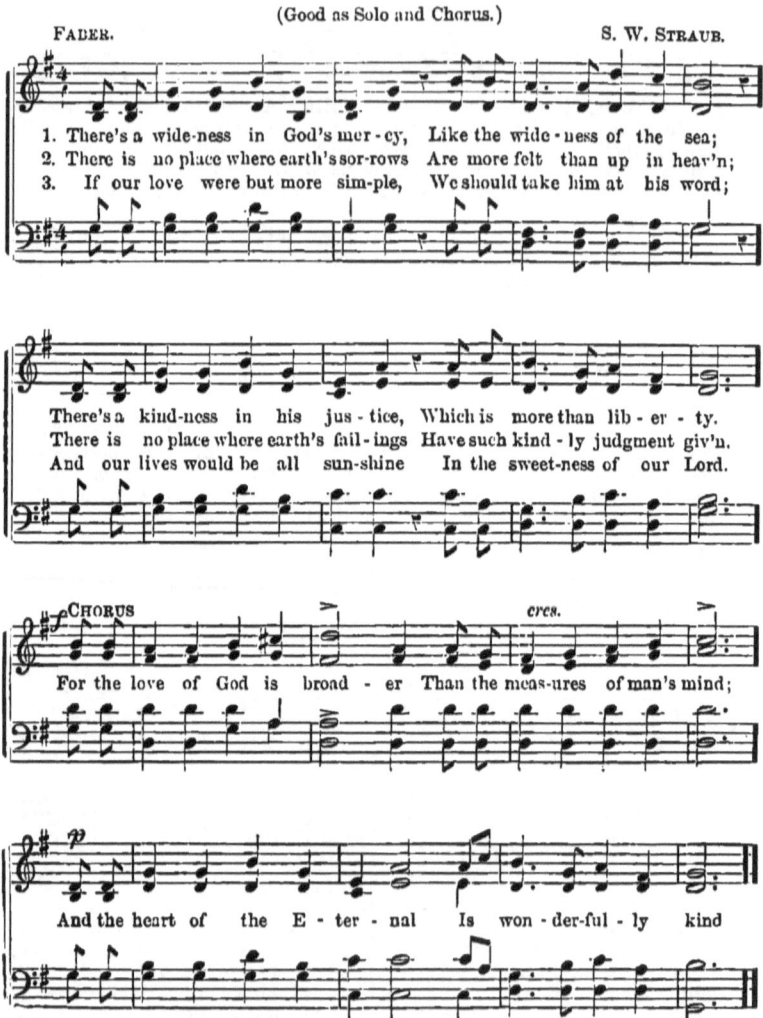

66 God's Love for Zion.

KELLY.   C. GOUNOD.

1. Zi-on stands with hills sur-round-ed—Zi-on, kept by power di-vine;
2. Ev-'ry hu-man tie may per-ish; Friend to friend un-faith-ful prove;
3. In the fur-nace God may prove thee, Thence to bring thee forth more bright,

All her foes shall be confound-ed, Though the world in arms com-bine;
Moth-ers cease their own to cher-ish; Heav'n and earth at last re-move;
But can nev-er cease to love thee; Thou art pre-cious in his sight:

Hap-py Zi-on, hap-py Zi-on, What a fa-vored lot is thine!
But no chang-es, but no chang-es Can at-tend Je-ho-vah's love.
God is with thee—God is with thee—God thine ev-er-last-ing light.

67   Tune, Lenox. (Key of B Flat.)

1. O, for a shout of joy
    Loud as the theme we sing!
  To this divine employ
    Your hearts and voices bring:
  Sound, sound, through all the earth abroad,
  The love, th'eternal love of God.

2. Unnumbered myriads stand,
    Of seraphs bright and fair,
  Or bow at his right hand,
    And pay their homage there;
  But strive in vain, with loudest chord,
  To sound the wondrous love of God.

GOD'S LOVE.

God is Love—Concluded.

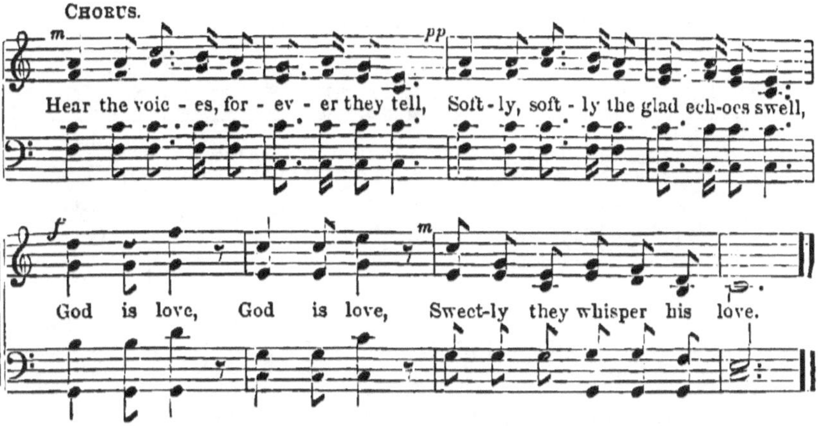

CHORUS.

Hear the voic - es, for - ev - er they tell, Soft - ly, soft - ly the glad ech-oes swell,

God is love, God is love, Sweet-ly they whisper his love.

70 Thou art My Shepherd.

M. E. THALHEIMER. Arr. from CRAMER.

1. Thou art my Shep - herd, Car - ing for all my need, Thy lit - tle lamb to feed. Trust - ing thee still, In the green pas-tures low, Where liv-ing wa-ters flow, Safe by thy side I go. Fear-ing no ill.
2. Or if my way lie Where death, o'er-hang-ing nigh, My soul would ter - ri - fy With sud - den chill, Yet I am not a - fraid: While soft-ly on my head Thy ten - der hand is laid, I Fear no ill.

GOD'S LOVE.

All Things are of God—Concluded.

Its glow by day, its smile by night, Are but re-flec-tions caught from thee;
And we can al - most think we gaze Thro' gold-en vis - tas in - to heav'n,
Like some dark, beauteous bird, whose plume Is sparkling with unnumbered eyes,—

Where'er we turn, thy glo - ries shine, And all things fair and bright are thine.
Those hues that mark the sun's de-cline, So soft, so radi-ant, Lord are thine.
That sa - cred gloom, those fires di - vine, So grand, so count-less, Lord, are thine.

Unbounded Love,
(ROCKINGHAM.)   MASON.

Great God! let all our tuneful powers A-wake and sing thy mighty name;
Sea - sons and moons, re - volv-ing round In beau-teous or - der, speak thy praise;
Each changing sea - son on our souls Its sweet-est kind - est influence sheds;
Our lives, our health, our friends, we owe, All to thy vast un-bound-ed love;

Thy hand rolls on our circl-ing hours; The hand from which our be - ing came.
And years, with smiling mercy crowned, To thee suc-ces - sive hon-ors raise.
And ev - 'ry per - iod, as it rolls, Showers countless blessings on our heads.
Ten thous-and prec-ious gifts be - low, And hope of no - bler joys a - bove.

CHRIST.

76. That Sweet Story of Old.

Mrs. JEMINA LUKE. ARTHUR BERRIDGE.

1. I think when I read that sweet sto-ry of old, When Je-sus was here a-mong men; How he called lit-tle children like lambs to his fold— I should like to have been with them then! I wish that his hands had been placed on my head, That his arms had been thrown around me; And that I might have
2. Yet still to his foot-stool in prayer I may go, And ask for a share in his love; And if I now earn-est-ly seek him be-low, I shall see him and hear him a-bove. In That beau-ti-ful place he has gone to pre-pare For all that are washed and for-giv'n, And ma-ny dear
3. But thousands and thousands who wan-der and fall, Never heard of that heav-en-ly home; I should like them to know there is room for them all, And that Je-sus has bid them to come, I long for the joy of that glo-ri-ous time, The sweet-est, and brightest, and best, When the dear lit-tle

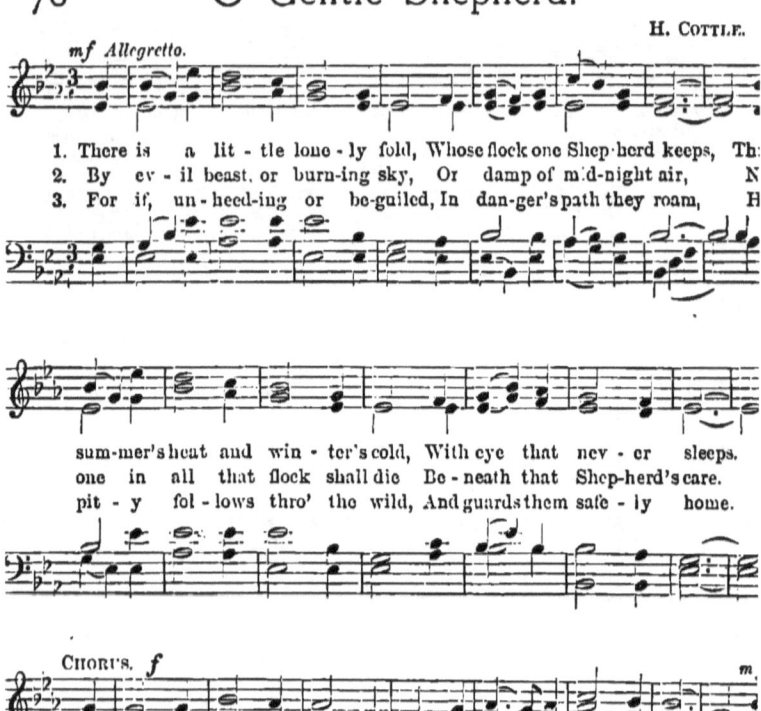

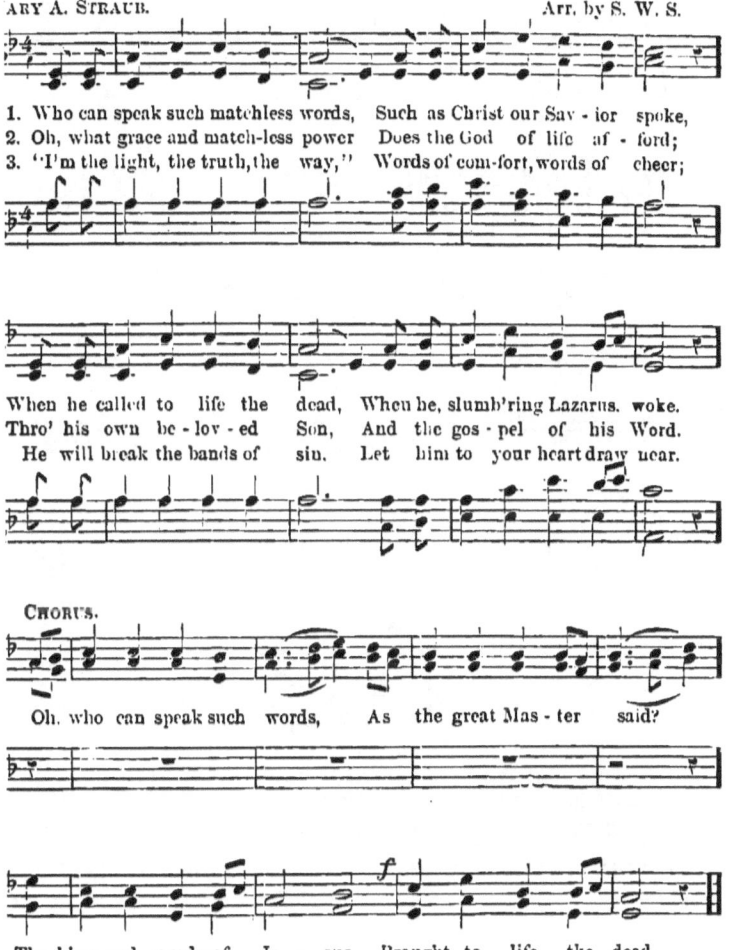

CHRIST.

Nearer to Thee—Concluded.

thee, for thou art my heav-en, Thou art my hope and my joy al-way.

81 Joy to the World.

D. WATTS. HANDEL.

1. Joy to the world the Lord is come! Let earth re-ceive her King;
2. Joy to the earth the Sav-ior reigns! Let men their songs em-ploy;
3. He rules the world with truth and grace, And makes the na-tions prove

Let ev-'ry heart pre-pare him room, And heav'n and na-ture sing, And
While fields, and floods, rocks, hills, and plains, Re-peat the sound-ing joy, Re-
The glo-ries of his right-eous-ness, And wonders of his love, And

heav'n and na-ture sing, And heav'n, And heav'n and na-ture sing.
peat the sounding joy, Re-peat, Re-peat the sound-ing joy,
won-ders of his love, And won- And won-ders of his love.
sing............ And heav'n and na-ture sing.

CHRIST.

83. Jesus, Make Me Holy.

mf Allegro. T. REED. Arr. by S. W. S.

1. Je-sus, make me ho-ly,   Make me use-ful, too;   I'll live for thy glo-ry,
2. Christ-like men are wanted, Who can stand and say, Which of you con-vin-ceth
3. Peo-ple who half-hearted, Are con-tent to be,   Are not used to bless those

Al-ways pure and true. All a-round the needs of   Ho-ly men I   see,
Me of sin to-day?" Oh thou Savior, cleanse me, Cleanse me thro' and thro',
Sunk in mis-er-y,   Those who live like Je-sus, Liv-ing but to   bless,

CHORUS.

Je-sus make me one of those Who live by lov-ing thee. More like thee, more like thee
And do make me pow'r for good In all God calls me to.
Joy and peace to souls they bear Deep down in wretchedness.

Make me, O my Sav-ior! More like thee, more like thee, That I may be thine a-lone.

84 Nearer the Cross.

88 The Master's Message.

JENNIE WILSON. S. W. STRAUB.

CHRIST.

The Master's Message—Concluded.

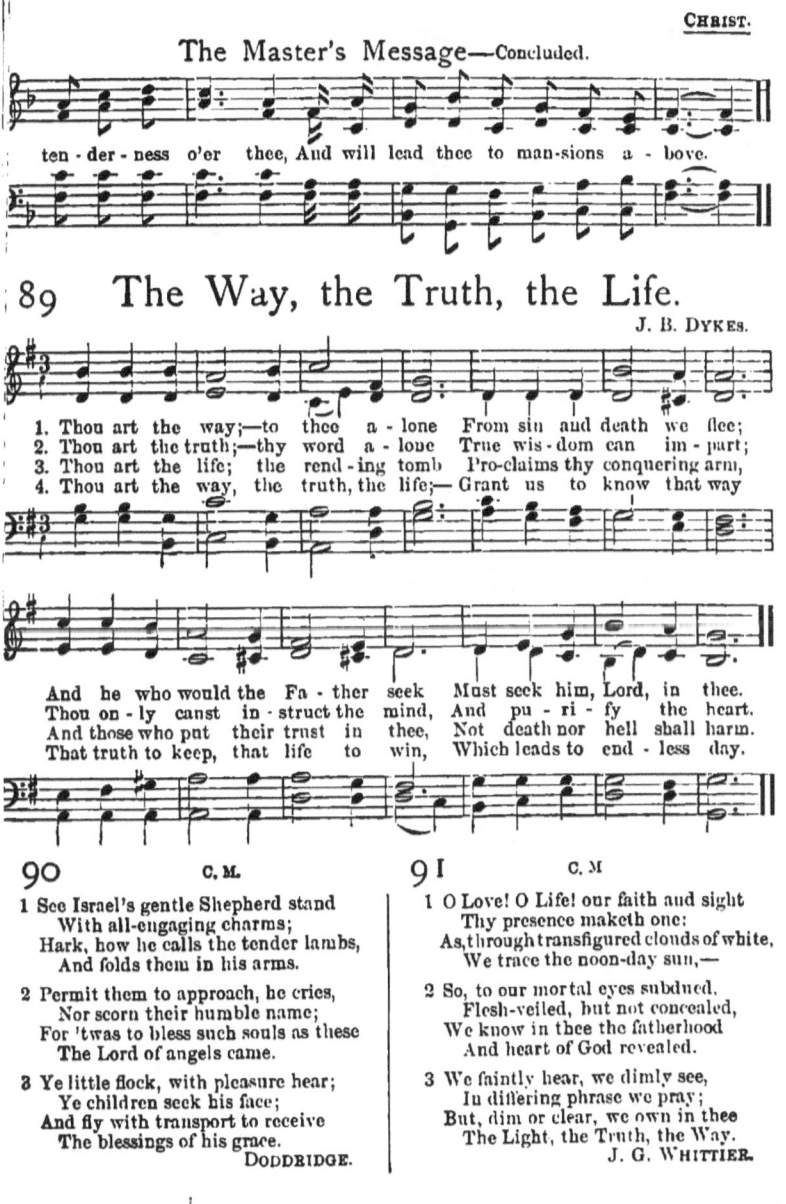

ten - der - ness o'er thee, And will lead thee to man-sions a - bove.

89 The Way, the Truth, the Life.
J. B. DYKES.

1. Thou art the way;—to thee a - lone From sin and death we flee;
2. Thou art the truth;—thy word a - lone True wis-dom can im - part;
3. Thou art the life; the rend-ing tomb Pro-claims thy conquering arm,
4. Thou art the way, the truth, the life;— Grant us to know that way

And he who would the Fa - ther seek Must seek him, Lord, in thee.
Thou on - ly canst in - struct the mind, And pu - ri - fy the heart.
And those who put their trust in thee, Not death nor hell shall harm.
That truth to keep, that life to win, Which leads to end - less day.

90 C. M.

1 See Israel's gentle Shepherd stand
  With all-engaging charms;
  Hark, how he calls the tender lambs,
  And folds them in his arms.

2 Permit them to approach, he cries,
  Nor scorn their humble name;
  For 'twas to bless such souls as these
  The Lord of angels came.

3 Ye little flock, with pleasure hear;
  Ye children seek his face;
  And fly with transport to receive
  The blessings of his grace.
                    DODDRIDGE.

91 C. M

1 O Love! O Life! our faith and sight
  Thy presence maketh one:
  As, through transfigured clouds of white,
  We trace the noon-day sun,—

2 So, to our mortal eyes subdued,
  Flesh-veiled, but not concealed,
  We know in thee the fatherhood
  And heart of God revealed.

3 We faintly hear, we dimly see,
  In differing phrase we pray;
  But, dim or clear, we own in thee
  The Light, the Truth, the Way.
                    J. G. WHITTIER.

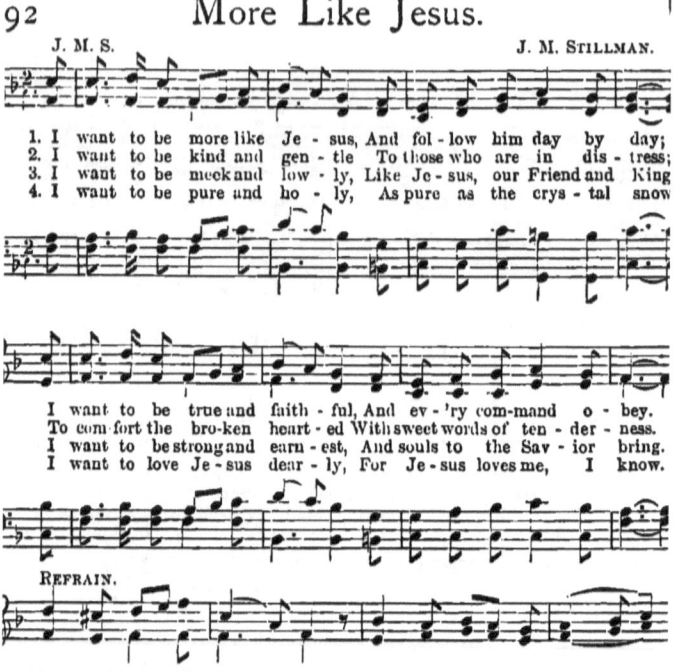

CHRIST.

93 Strong Son of God.

TENNYSON. Arr. by W. H. MONK.

1. Strong Son of God, im-mor-tal love, Whom we, that have not seen thy face,
2. Thou seem-est hu-man and di-vine, The high-est, ho-liest man-hood, thou:
3. Our lit-tle sys-tems have their day; They have their day and cease to be;

By faith, and faith a-lone, em-brace, Be-liev-ing where we can-not prove!
Our wills are ours, we know not how, Our wills are ours, to make them thine.
They are but bro-ken lights of thee, And thou, O Lord, art more than they.

94   L. M.

1 Teach us to feel as Jesus prayed,
  When on the cross he bleeding hung;
  When all his foes their wrath displayed,
  And with their spite his bosom stung.

2 Till death, he loved his foes, and said,
  "Father, forgive,"—then groaned and died;
  And when arisen from the dead,
  His mercy to their souls applied.

3 For such a heart and such a love,
  O Lord, we raise our prayer to thee;
  Oh, pour thy Spirit from above,
  That we may like our Savior be.

95   L. M.

1 Come, Savior, Jesus, from above,
  Assist me with thy heavenly grace;
  Empty my heart of earthly love,
  And for thyself prepare the place.

2 Oh, let thy sacred presence fill,
  And set my longing spirit free;
  Which pants to have no other will,
  But night and day to live for thee.

3 Henceforth may no profane delight
  Divide this consecrated soul;
  Possess it thou, who hast the right,
  As Lord and Master of the whole.

96

Key of F.

1 What a friend we have in Jesus,
  All our sins and griefs to bear!
  What a privilege to carry
  Everything to God in prayer!
  O, what peace we often forfeit,
  O, what needless pain we bear,
  All because we do not carry
  Everything to God in prayer.

2 Have we trials and temptations?
  Is there trouble anywhere?
  We should never be discouraged,—
  Take it to the Lord in prayer.
  Can we find a friend so faithful,
  Who will all our sorrows share?
  Jesus knows our every weakness—
  Take it to the Lord in prayer.
        HORATIUS BONAR.

THE CHRIST.

Sing of Jesus' Love—Concluded.

cheers the soul in times of need, And al-lays our ev-'ry fear.

98 Lord and Master of us All.

J. G. WHITTIER.   J. B. DYKES.

1. Im-mor-tal Love, for-ev-er full, For-ev-er flow-ing free,
2. We may not climb the heav'-nly steeps To bring the Lord Christ down:
3. But warm, sweet, ten-der, e-ven yet A pres-ent help is He;
4. Thro' Him the first fond prayr's are said Our lips of childhood frame,
5. O Lord and Mas-ter of us all! What-e'er our name or sign,

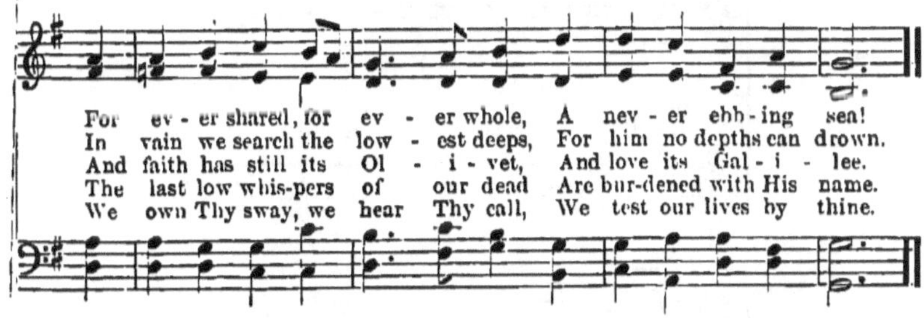

For ev-er shared, for ev-er whole, A nev-er ebb-ing sea!
In vain we search the low-est deeps, For him no depths can drown.
And faith has still its Ol-i-vet, And love its Gal-i-lee.
The last low whis-pers of our dead Are bur-dened with His name.
We own Thy sway, we hear Thy call, We test our lives by thine.

---

99   Key of G.

1 All hail the power of Jesus' name,
  Let angels prostrate fall;
  Bring forth the royal diadem,
    And crown him Lord of all.

2 Let every kindred, every tribe
  On this terrestrial ball,
  To him all majesty ascribe,
    And crown him Lord of all.

3 Oh, that with yonder sacred throng
  We at his feet may fall!
  We'll join the everlasting song,
    And crown him Lord of all.

100   Key of G.

1 Oh, for a thousand tongues to sing,
  My great Redeemer's praise,
  The glories of my Lord and King,
    The triumphs of his grace!

2 Jesus the name that charms our fears,
  That bids our sorrow cease,—
  'Tis music in the sinner's ears,
    'Tis life, and health, and peace.

3 He speaks,and, listening to his voice,
  New life the dead receive;
  The mournful, broken hearts rejoice,
    The humble poor believe.

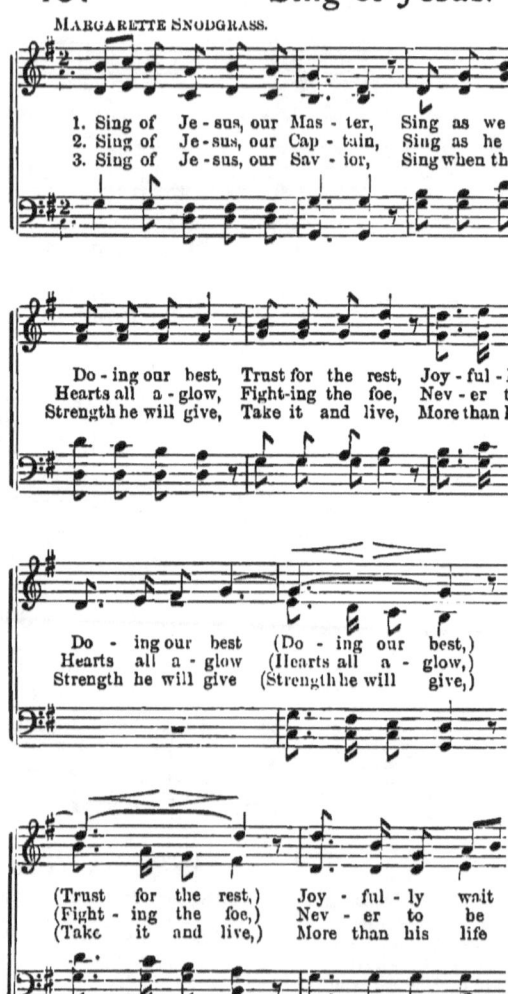

CHRIST.

102 In the Cross of Christ I Glory.

ROBERT SCHUMANN. Arr. by S. W. S.

1. In the cross of Christ I glo - ry, Towering o'er the wreck of time;
2. When the woes of life o'er - take me, Hopes de-ceive, and fears an - noy,
3. When the sun of bliss is beam - ing Light and love up - on my way,
4. Bane and bless-ing, pain and pleas - ure, By the cross are sanc - ti - fied;

All the light of sa - cred sto - ry, Gathers round its head sub-lime.
Nev - er shall the cross for - sake me; Lo! it glows with peace and joy.
From the cross the ra-diance streaming, Adds new lus - ter to the day.
Peace is there, that knows no meas - ure, Joys that thro' all time a - bide.

103 Longing for Christ.

Rev. J. J. HAMILTON. S. W. STRAUB.
Rather fast.

1. Lord! I de - sire with thee to dwell, With thee to walk each day:
2. Still near - er, near - er, draw my soul; Still bright-er show thy face;
3. O! let my heart be wholly thine, And thine my life and death:

# 104 Give Us Enduring Faith.

MARIA STRAUB. S. W. STRAUB.

1. The God of wis-dom, God of love, We own his pow'r and sway,
Yet fear to trust his hand to guide Us through the des - ert way;
For - give us Lord, 'tis sin we own, To ev - er doubt thy word,
We know the guid-ance is di - vine; Thy prom - ise we have heard.

2. Cre - a - tion all is in his hands, He made and he main - tains;
His chil - dren know and feel the pow'r That won-drous-ly sus-tains;
He guides the guid - ing star, that points For us the way, the life;
Wher-e'er the beauteous beams il - lume, Is all with bless-ings rife.

3. O for a faith that will en - dure Thro' sun and shade the same,
To trust our Fa-ther as the child That can but lisp the name;
Thou might - y One of pow'r di - vine, With love and wis-dom fraught
Help us to love thee and o - bey, And trust thee as we ought.

FAITH AND TRUST.

105 Choose Thou for Me, my God.

BONAR.   BARNBY.

1. Thy way, not mine, O Lord, How-ev-er dark it be!
2. I dare not choose my lot: I would not, if I might;
3. The king-dom that I seek Is thine: so let the way
4. Not mine, not mine the choice, In things or great or small;

Lead me by thine own hand; Choose out the path for me.
Choose thou for me, my God, So shall I walk a-right.
That leads to it be Thine, Else I must sure-ly stray.
Be Thou my Guide, my Strength, My Wis-dom and my All.

106 The Pure in Heart.

Dr. J. M. NEALE.   Arr. by S. W. STRAUB.

1. Bless-ed are the pure in heart: They have loved the bet-ter part,
2. Till in glo-ry they ap-pear, They shall oft-en see Him here;
3. When the sun be-gins to rise, Spread-ing brightness thro' the skies,
4. God in ev-'ry thing they see; First in all their thoughts is he.

When life's jour-ney they have trod, They shall go to see their God.
And his grace shall learn to know In his glo-rious work be-low.
They will love to praise and bless Christ, the Sun of Right-eous-ness.
They have loved the bet-ter part; Bless-ed are the pure in heart.

FAITH AND TRUST.

107 God is Near Thee.

JESSICA RANKIN.   SMART. Arr. by S. W. S.

DUET. Soprano and Contralto. *Andantino.*

1. Faint not, fear not, God is near thee, Tho' thou dost for-get his love; Bring thy sor-rows, he will hear thee, From his heav'n-ly throne a-bove; Oft-en as thou hast of-fend-ed Bless-ings still thy life doth
2. Clouds may veil the light of morn-ing, Storms ob-scure the sun's warm rays. Faint not, mist at ear-ly dawn-ing Oft for-tell a glo-rious day; Let no threat'ning clouds op-press thee, He can make the dark-ness

CONTRALTO.

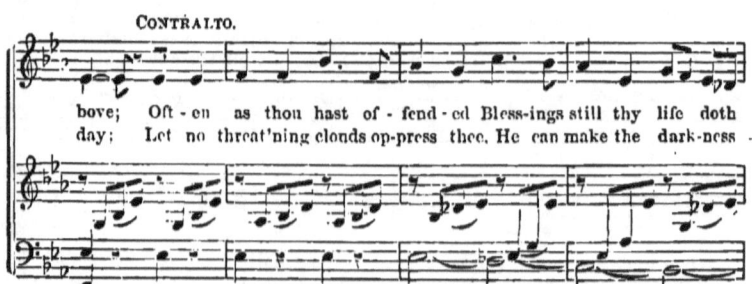

108 Give Me the Faith of a Child.

MARIA STRAUB.   HAROLD B. ADAMS.

1. Fa-ther, for-give, if' thy good-ness I grieve, When I come ask-ing, but do not be-lieve; Give me, O give me the faith of a child, Sim-ple and rest-ful, en-dur-ing and mild.
2. When I am wea-ry, op-press'd or dis-trest, Glad - ly I think of the prom-ise of rest; When I be-lieve, then my Sav-ior comes near, Takes all my bur-dens, and gives me his cheer.
3. Fa-ther, I own thee, O make me thy child, Trust-ful and du-ti-ful, pure, un-de-filed; Guard me and keep me, and make me to be, Worth-y thy Fa-ther-ly care o-ver me.

FAITH AND TRUST.

Give Me the Faith of a Child—Concluded.

give............ me the faith............... of a child...............
faith of a child, Give me, dear Fa - ther, the faith of a child.

109 Wait and Trust.

HAVERGAL. RANDEGGER. Arr. by S. W. S.

1. Sad - ly bend the flow - ers, In the heav - y rain: Af - ter beating
2. When a sud-den sor - row Comes like cloud and night, Wait for God's to-

show-ers, Sunbeams come a - gain. Lit - tle birds are sil - ent All the dark night
mor - row; All will then be bright. On - ly wait and trust him Just a lit - tle

111   He is My Rock.

Mrs. BELLE TOWNE   J. M. STILLMAN, by per.

FAITH AND TRUST.

SOLO, ad lib.   CHORUS.

1. If thy path is like night, Then trust in the Lord, For
2. If thy jour-ney is long, Then trust in the Lord, For
3. If thy bur-dens bear down, Then trust in the Lord, For
4. There is strength for each day, So trust in the Lord, For

SOLO, ad lib.

he is our rock and sal-va-tion; You must stand for the right, And
he is our rock and sal-va-tion; Cheer the heart with a song, And
he is our rock and sal-va-tion; Let the world see no frown, But
he is our rock and sal-va-tion; Do not turn from the way, But

CHORUS.

trust in the Lord, For he is our rock and sal-va-tion; For
trust in the Lord,
trust in the Lord,
trust in the Lord,

he is our rock, for he is our rock, for he is our rock and sal-va-tion.

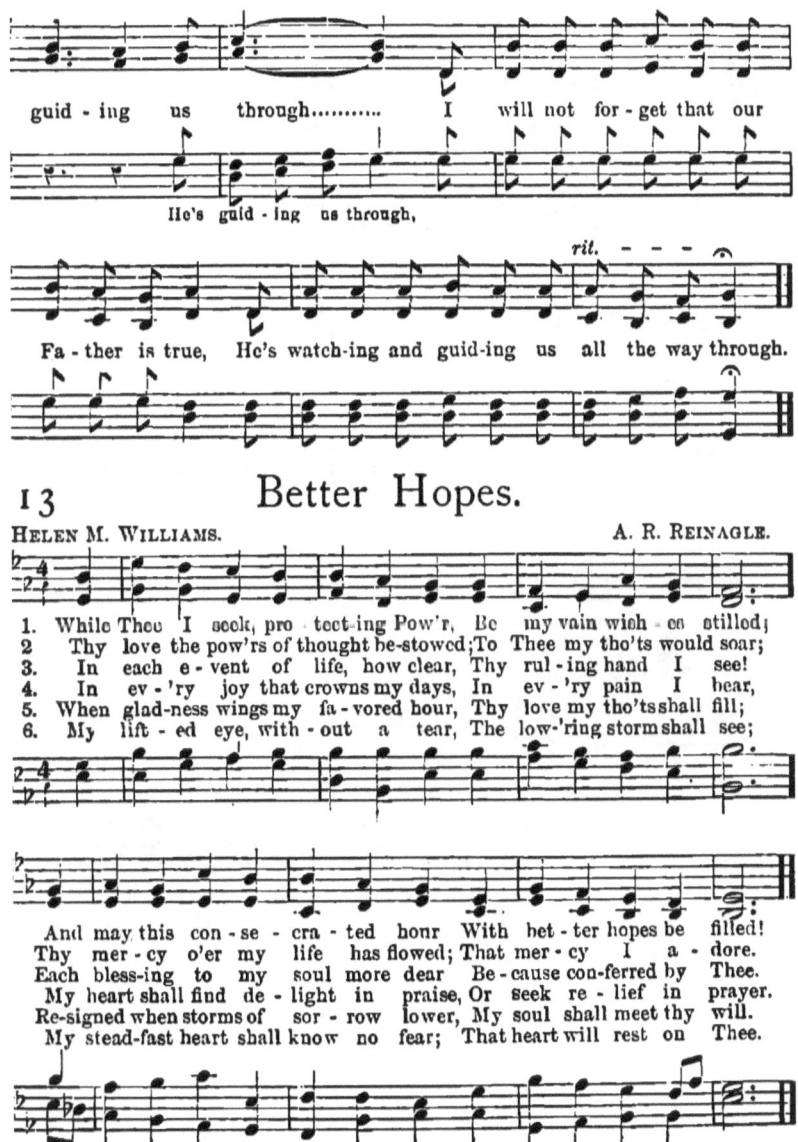

FAITH AND TRUST.

114 On What are You Building?

E. E. REXFORD L. S. EDWARDS, by per.

1. Are you build-ing your house on the sand, brother? To-day may be
2. The house that is built on the rock, brother, No tem-pest of
3. Let the rock that you build your house on, brother, Be Je-sus the

sun-ny and fair, But the mor-row may bring us the tem-pest, brother,
earth can o'er-throw, While you're building, build safely and sure-ly, brother,
hope of us all; The house built on this steadfast foun-da-tion, brother,

CHORUS.

So choose your foundation with care.   Let us build on the rock, ev-er
On the rock that is steadfast below.
Will stand when the mountains shall fall.

build on the rock, While the storms of life are rag-ing, Let us

God our Help.

ARTHUR COTTMAN.

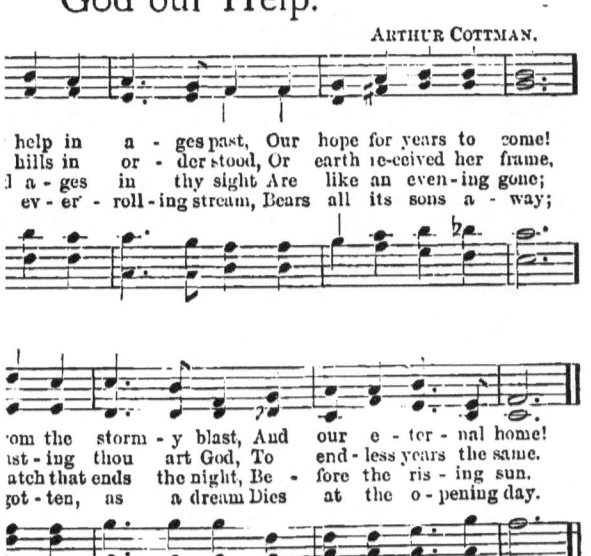

help in a - ges past, Our hope for years to come!
hills in or - der stood, Or earth re-ceived her frame,
] a - ges in thy sight Are like an even-ing gone;
ev - er - roll-ing stream, Bears all its sons a - way;

'om the storm - y blast, And our e - ter - nal home!
ıst - ing thou art God, To end - less years the same.
atch that ends the night, Be - fore the ris - ing sun.
ɡot - ten, as a dream Dies at the o - pening day.

FAITH AND TRUST.

Portuguese Hymn.

JOHN READING.

117

1 How firm a foundation, ye saints of the
  Lord! [word!
 Is laid for your faith in his excellent
 What more can he say than to you he
  hath said,—
 To you, who for refuge to Jesus have fled?

2 "Fear not, I am with thee; oh, be not dis-
  mayed, [aid:
 For I am thy God, I will still give thee
 I'll strengthen thee, help thee, and cause
  thee to stand,
 Upheld by my gracious, omnipotent hand.

3 "When through fiery trials thy pathway
  shall lie, [ply,
 My grace, all-sufficient, shall be thy sup-
 The flame shall not hurt thee; I only de-
  sign [refine."
 Thy dross to consume, and thy gold to
    KIRKHAM.

118

1 The Lord is our Shepherd, our Guardian
  and Guide;
 Whatever we want he will kindly provide;
 His care and protection his flock will sur-
  round;
 To them will his mercies forever abound.

2 The Lord is our Shepherd; what, then,
  shall we fear? [near?
 Shall dangers affrighten us while he is
 O, no: when he calls us we'll walk through
  the vale, [not fail.
 The shadow of death, but our hearts shall

3 The Lord is become our salvation and
  song, [long;
 His blessings have followed us all our life
 His name will we praise, while he lends
  to us breath, [our death.
 Be joyful through life, and resigned in
    BYROM.

FAITH AND TRUST.

Under the Shadow of Thy Wings—Concluded.

120   Tune, Ortonville. (Key of B Flat.)

1 We wait in faith, in prayer we wait,
   Until the happy hour
 When God shall ope the morning gate,
   By his almighty power.

2 We wait in faith, and turn our face
   To where the daylight springs;
 Till he shall come earth's gloom to chase,
   With healing on his wings.

3 And even now, amid the gray,
   The east is brightening fast,
 And kindling to that perfect day,
   Which never shall be past.

4 We wait in faith, we wait in prayer,
   Till that blest day shall shine,
 When earth shall fruits of Eden bear,
   And all, O God, be thine!

FAITH AND TRUST.

Where He Leads I'll Follow—Concluded.

122 Arlington.
Key of G.

1 The wrong that pains my soul below
  I dare not throne above:
  I know not of His hate.—I know
  His goodness and his love.

2 I dimly guess from blessings known
  Of greater out of sight,
  And, with the chastened Psalmist, own
  His judgments, too, are right.

3 No offering of my own, I have,
  Nor works my faith to prove;
  I can but give the gifts he gave
  And plead his love for love.

4 O brothers! if my faith is vain,
  If hopes like these betray,
  Pray for me that my feet may gain
  The sure and safer way.
                              WHITTIER.

123 Balerma
Key of A.

1 Jehovah God! thy gracious power
  On every hand we see;
  O may the blessings of each hour
  Lead all our thoughts to thee.

2 If, on the wings of morn, we speed
  To earth's remotest bound,
  Thy hand will there our footsteps lead,
  Thy love our path surround.

3 Thy power is in the ocean deeps,
  And reaches to the skies;
  Thine eye of mercy never sleeps,
  Thy goodness never dies.

4 In all the varying scenes of time,
  On thee our hopes depend;
  Through every age, in every clime,
  Our Father and our Friend.
                              THOMPSON.

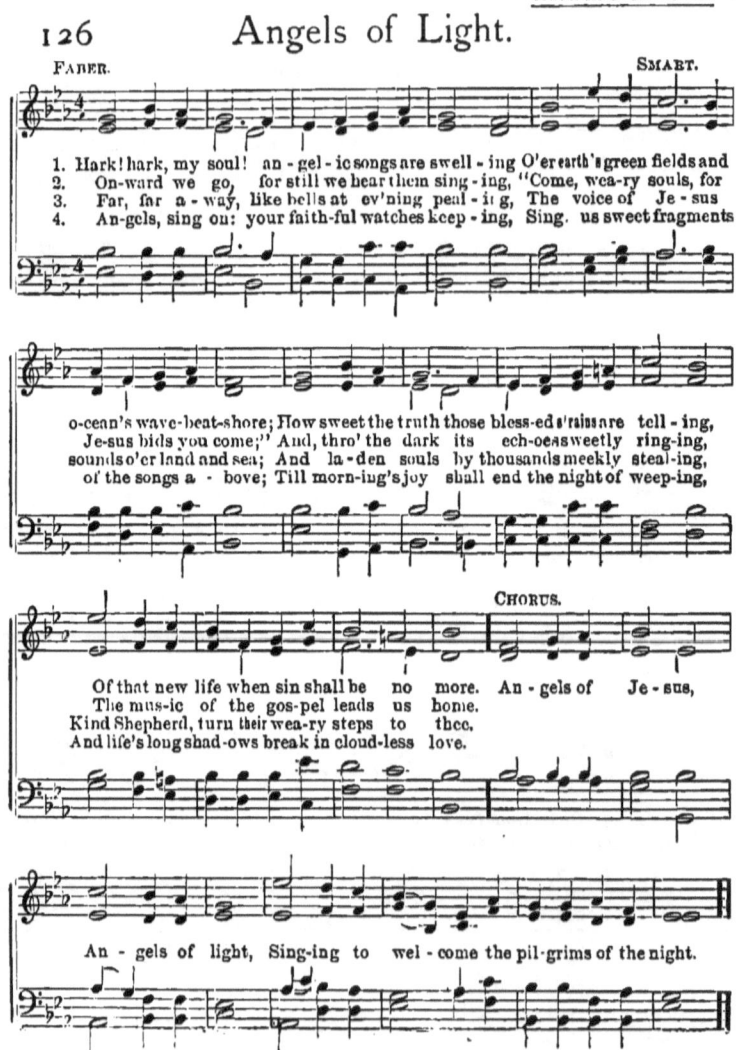

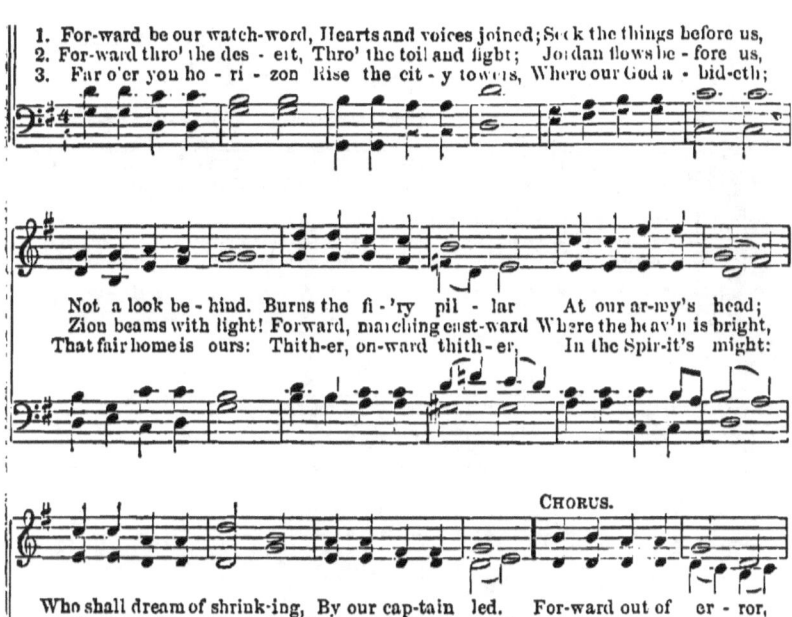

HOPE AND COURAGE.

133. Press on to win the prize.

ARTHUR BERRIDGE.

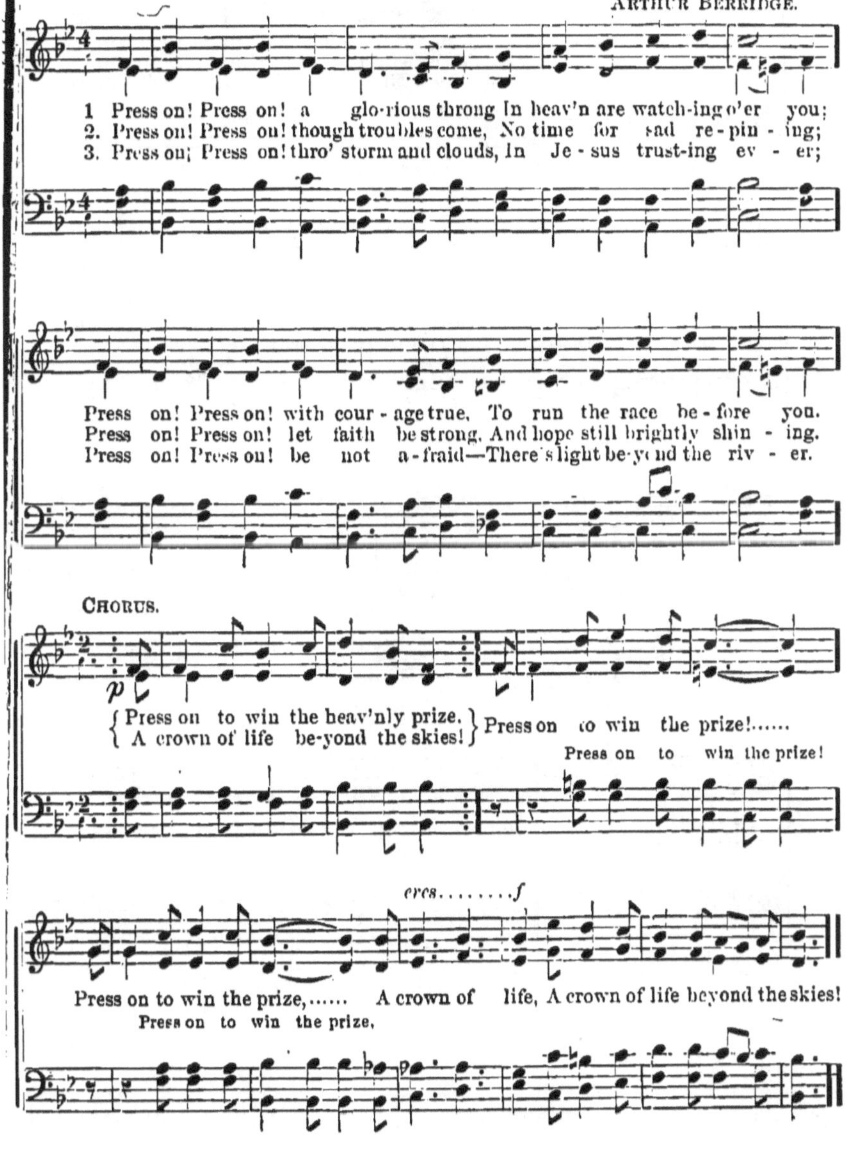

1 Press on! Press on! a glorious throng In heav'n are watching o'er you;
2. Press on! Press on! though troubles come, No time for sad repining;
3. Press on! Press on! thro' storm and clouds, In Jesus trusting ever;

Press on! Press on! with courage true, To run the race before you.
Press on! Press on! let faith be strong, And hope still brightly shining.
Press on! Press on! be not afraid—There's light beyond the river.

CHORUS.

p

{ Press on to win the heav'nly prize. } Press on to win the prize!......
{ A crown of life beyond the skies! }
Press on to win the prize!

cres........f

Press on to win the prize,...... A crown of life, A crown of life beyond the skies!
Press on to win the prize,

134. Will You Stand up for Jesus?

Rev. M. LOWRIE HOFFORD, D. D.
W. A. OGDEN, by per.

1. Will you stand up for Je-sus? Will you stand in his might? Will you gird on his ar-mor, and be first in the fight? Will you trust in his prom-ise? Shall his s'rength make you strong? Shall the dear name of Je-sus be your watch-word and song?

2. Will you stand up for Je-sus With a heart that is true? Will you stand up for Je-sus, who hath borne much for you? Will you trust in his mer-cy, In his strength be made strong? Shall the dear name of Je-sus be your watch-word and song?

3. Will you stand up for Je-sus Till the con-flict is o'er? Till the bu-gle is sound-ing in your hear-ing no more? Till the dawn of the morn-ing Meets in tri-umph your eyes? And the pæ-ans of vic-t'ry sound a-loud in the skies?

CHORUS.

Will you stand, will you stand with a heart firm and true?

136. Always Speak the Truth.

J. W. PRATT.

1. Be the matter what it may, Always speak the truth;
2. There's a charm in verity; Always speak the truth;
3. Falsehood seldom stands alone, Always speak the truth;

Whether work, or whether play, Always speak the truth.
But there's meanness in a lie, Always speak the truth.
One begets another one, Always speak the truth.

Never from this rule depart; Grave it deeply on your heart;
He is but a coward slave, Who, a present pain to waive,
Falsehood all the soul degrades, Stains with sin and ever breeds

Written 'tis on virtue's chart, Always speak the truth.
Stoops to falsehood; then he brave; Always speak the truth.
Evil thoughts and darker deeds; Always speak the truth.

137. Light from the Heights Beyond.

M.
S. W. Straub.

1. Pass - ing thro' the low - ly val - ley, Pil - grim, ne'er de - spond;
2. There is safe - ty in the val - ley, Walk - ing in the light;
3. Pass - ing thro' death's dreaded val - ley, Dimm'd your earth - ly sight;

See, O see the gold - en g'eam - ing, From the heights be - yond.
Je - sus is the light from heav - en, Beam - ing thro' the night.
Cheer up, see the heights of glo - ry, Melt - ing in - to light.

Chorus. *Faster.*

Light is gleam - ing, bright - ly gleam - ing, From the heights be - yond;

Chris - tian, fear not, light is beam - ing, From the heights be - yond.
Chris - tian, fear not, light is beam - ing, From the heights be - yond.

HOPE AND COURAGE.

138. Be Not Afraid.

MARY A. STRAUB. S. W. S.

1. O turn to-ward Zi - on, thou lone, wea - ry one;
2. Press on, wea - ry pil - grim, and do not dis - may;
3. Be stead - fast and faint not, tho' foes may as - sail,

Though rug - ged thy path - way, thou'rt journ'y - ing tow'rd home,
The night will grow short - er and bright - er the day;
Temp - ta - tions o'er-whelm thee, and storm - clouds pre - vail;

The face of thy Fa - ther, maj - es - tic, sub - lime,
The sun, ev - er glo - rious, will shine thro' thy tears,
Thy Fa - ther is near thee with strong lov - ing arm,

Il - lu - mines thy foot - steps with ra - diance di - vine.
Will scat - ter the dark - ness and ban - ish thy fears.
To shield and pro - tect thee and keep thee from harm.

HOPE AND COURAGE.

Be Not Afraid—Concluded.

Be not a-fraid, be not a-fraid, The light is shin-ing for thee,
is shining for thee.

Be not a-fraid, be not a-fraid: Thy Fa-ther is near to thee.

---

139 Webb.
Key of B Flat.

1 Stand up!—stand up for Jesus!
  The trumpet call obey:
  Forth to the mighty conflict,
  In this his glorious day:
  "Yet that are men, now serve him,"
  Against unnumbered foes;
  Your courage rise with danger,
  And strength to strength oppose.

2 Stand up!—stand up for Jesus!
  Stand in his strength alone;
  The arm of flesh will fail you,
  Ye dare not trust your own:
  Put on the gospel armor,
  And, watching unto prayer,
  Where duty calls, or danger,
  Be never wanting there.

3 Stand up!—stand up for Jesus!
  The strife will not be long;
  This day the noise of battle,
  The next the victor's song:
  To him that overcometh,
  A crown of life shall be;
  He with the King of Glory
  Shall reign eternally!

140 Boylston.
Key of D.

1 Give to the winds thy fears;
  Hope, and be undismayed;
  God hears thy sighs, God counts thy tears;
  God shall lift up thy head.

2 Through waves, through clouds, and storms;
  He gently clears thy way;
  Wait thou his time, so shall the night
  Soon end in joyous day.

3 He everywhere hath rule,
  And all things serve his might:
  His every act pure blessing is,
  His path unsullied light.

4 Thou seest our weakness, Lord,
  Our hearts are known to thee:
  Oh, lift thou up the sinking hand,
  Confirm thee feeble knee!

5 Let us, in life or death,
  Boldly thy truth declare;
  And publish, with our latest breath,
  Thy love and guardian care,

141. Onward, Day by Day.

HOPE AND COURAGE.

MARIA STRAUB.   S. W. STRAUB.

Firmly. Not too fast.

1. On-ward, onward, onward, onward day by day, Fear-ing not the dan-ger
2. On-ward, onward, onward, tho' the way be drear, There is some-thing still a-
3. On-ward, onward, onward, tho' the foe be strong, Fear not, be your mot-to

ly - ing 'long the way; Are you in the val - ley or up-on the steeps?
long the way to cheer; Oft as comes the night-time, comes the beauteous day
striving 'gainst the wrong Pa - tient ev - er help-ing, oth - ers at your side,

CHORUS.

Trust in Him to guide you, He who never sleeps. Marching along! marching alon
There are blessings ev'ry-where a-long life's way.
Trust in God, who nev - er-fail - ing will provide.

On-ward marching day by day; Are you in the val - ley or

HOPE AND COURAGE.

Onward, Day by Day—Concluded.

on the mountain high, Trust in God to keep you, he is ev - er nigh

142 There's Light Above the Clouds.

M. A. S. MARY A. STRAUB.

Cheerfully.

1. There's light a-bove the clouds, bright and clear; A strong arm leads you
2. The temp - est brings a calm all se - rene; Spring show - ers bring the
3. The light of life is truth from a - bove; True glad - ness in the

CHORUS.

on, do not fear. Then look up - ward, ev - er up-ward, There is
grass, fresh and green.
heart is God's love.

Repeat last time pp.

light pure and bright, Ev - er shin - ing, pure and bright.
ev - er shin-ing, pure and bright.

WORK.

Mighty to Save.—Concluded.

Chorus.

Might-y to save, might-y to save, Say ye to the daughter of Zi - on,

Might-y to save, might-y to save, Je - sus Christ is might-y to save.

144 We do it Unto Thee.

W. W. How.
Arr. from SCHUMANN.

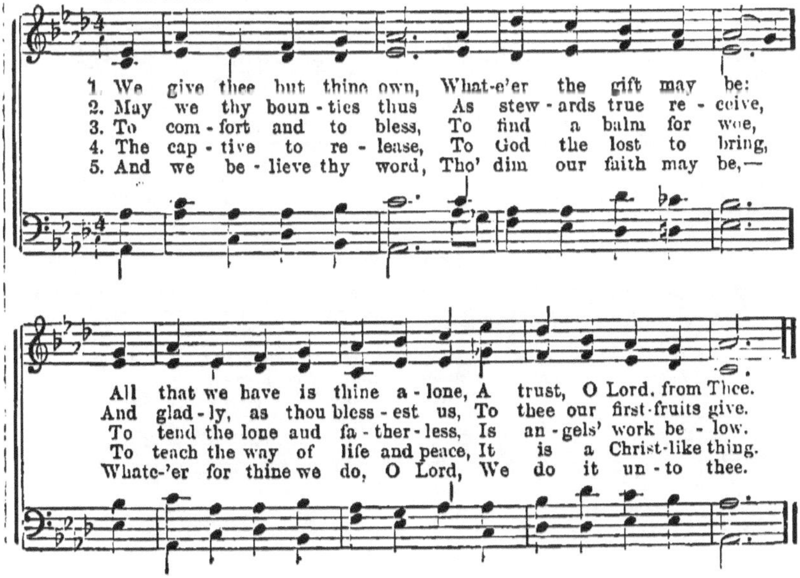

1. We give thee but thine own, What-e'er the gift may be:
2. May we thy boun-ties thus As stew-ards true re - ceive,
3. To com-fort and to bless, To find a balm for woe,
4. The cap-tive to re - lease, To God the lost to bring,
5. And we be - lieve thy word, Tho' dim our faith may be,—

All that we have is thine a - lone, A trust, O Lord, from Thee.
And glad-ly, as thou bless-est us, To thee our first-fruits give.
To tend the lone and fa - ther - less, Is an - gels' work be - low.
To teach the way of life and peace, It is a Christ-like thing.
Whate-'er for thine we do, O Lord, We do it un - to thee.

145 Forth to the Rescue Go.

WORK.
HILL.

1. Praise the Lord, we now are free! Christ has brought us lib-er-ty!
2. There's a balm for ev-'ry wound In the Sav-ior to be found;
3. See, our Ar-my's marching on, O'er the re-gions far and near;

In the ar-my brave we march to save Men from sin's slav-e-ry.
At the cross in pray'er he'll meet us there, And make our peace a-bound.
We a-gainst each foe will brave-ly go, Our hearts shall know no fear.

See the count-less mil-lions die! Hear their groans of deep-est woe!
At the cross there's room for all Who will at his foot-stool fall;
And when crowns of earth shall fade, And its glo-ries pass a-way,

Je-sus calls to you, his sol-diers true, "Forth to the res-cue go!"
There is peace and joy with-out al-loy, Come, heed his lov-ing call.
We'll re-joice and sing to Christ our King, Thro' one e-ter-nal day.

WORK.

Forth to the Rescue Go—Concluded.

CHORUS.

March on! We shall win the day! March on! Hear the Sav-ior say,

"March on till the vic-t'ry's won, Then you shall hear the glad, "Well done!"

146 More Labor for the Lord.

SAMUEL LONGFELLOW. H. J. GAUNTLETT.

1. Oh, still in ac cents sweet and strong Sounds forth the an-cient word,
2. We hear the call; in dreams no more In self - ish ease we lie,
3. Where proph-ets' word, and mar-tyrs' blood, And prayers of saints were sown,
4. O thou whose call our hearts has stirred! To do thy will we come;

"More reap - ers for white har - vest fields, More la - borers for the Lord!"
But gird - ed for our Fa - ther's work, Go forth beneath His sky.
We, to their la - bors entering in, Would reap where they have strown.
Thrust in our sick - les at thy word, And bear our har - vest home.

WORK.

Sowing the Seed of the Kingdom—Concluded.

will you gar - ner an - y, For the gath-'ring at the har - vest home?

148. Servants of Christ, Arise.

L. H. SIGOURNEY.   Arr. from BEETHOVEN.

1. Ser - vants of Christ, a - rise, And gird you for the toil;
2. Go where the sick re - cline, Where mourn-ing hearts de - plore;

The dew of prom-ise from the skies Al - read - y cheers the soil.
And where the sons of sor - row pine, Dis-pense your hal-lowed lore.

3 Urge, with a tender zeal,
   The erring child along,
Where peaceful congregations kneel,
   And pious teachers throng.

4 Be faith, which looks above,
   With prayer, your constant guest,
And wrap the Savior's changeless love
   A mantle round your breast.

5 So shall you share the wealth,
   That earth may ne'er despoil,
And the blest gospel's saving health
   Repay your arduous toil.

149. On, to the Field.

MARIA STRAUB. Arr. by. S. W. S.

mf Allegro moderato.

1. Go forth to the har-vest field, (the harvest field,) Help gath-er the gold-en yield; (the golden yield,) The Sav-ior calls you, hear him say, "Go work to-day."
2. Go work, for the field is white, (the field is white,) Go bold-ly to do the right, (to do the right,) O dread it not, each coming morn The work be-gin.
3. Go forth to the har-vest field, (the harvest field,) Go brave-ly the reap-er wield, (the reaper wield,) Help gar-ner in the pre-cious store, From ru-in save.

March on-ward, be brave, have cour-age to do The Lord's bless-ed will al-way.
The la-b'rers are few, there's much you can do, A-rise, help the good to glean.
The sheaves must be bound, there's e-vil around, March on to the field, be brave.

150. Go Work To-Day.

BONAR.   BEETHOVEN.

1. Go, labor on; spend and be spent, Thy joy to do the Father's will:
2. Go, labor on; 'tis not for naught; Thine earthly loss is heav'n-ly gain:
3. Go, labor on; e-nough while here, If he shall praise thee; if he deign

It is the way the Master went; Should not the servant tread it still?
Men heed thee, love thee. praise thee not; The Master prais-es, what are men?
Thy willing heart to mark and cheer, No toil for him shall be in vain.

151

1 Press on, press on! ye sons of light,
Untiring in your holy fight,
Still treading each temptation down,
And battling for a brighter crown.

2 Press on, press on! through toil and woe,
With calm resolve. to triumph go,
And make each dark and threatening ill
Yield but a higher glory still.

3 Press on, press on! still look in faith
To him who vanquished sin and death;
Then shall ye hear God's word, "Well done!"
True to the last, press on, press on!

152

1 The Christian warrior, see him stand
In the whole armor of his God;
The Spirit's sword is in his hand;
His feet are with the gospel shod.

2. In panoply of truth complete,
Salvation's helmet on his head,
With righteousness a breastplate meet,
And faith's broad shield before him spread.

3 Thus strong in his Redeemer's strength
Sin, death, and hell he tramples down,— [lengtht
Fights the good fight; and takes a,
Through mercy, an immortal crown.

The Trumpet's Call to War—Concluded.

Brave sol-diers of Christ we'll prove we are, By glad-ly standing firm for Je - sus;
Ral-ly-ing round the banner of our Sav - - ior, We're a might-y
round the ban - ner of our Sav - ior,
ar - my, all e quipp'd for the fight; Stead - i - ly on-ward, shoul-der close to
Stead - i - ly on - ward, ev - er on - ward,
shoul - - der, We will march to win the world for Je - sus.
shoul - der close to shoul-der,

154 Marching at the King's Command.

MARIA STRAUB. S. W. STRAUB.

Marching at the King's Command.—Concluded.

WORK.

bless-ed the re - ward, Grand - ly march-ing in the ar - my of the Lord.

155 Better than Gold.

LUELLA CLARK. Arr. from REINECKE, by S. W. S.

DUET. *mf*

1. Speak kind-ly, speak kind-ly, to young and to old: The words of true
2. Speak kind-ly, speak kind-ly; no tongue can ex-press The pow'r of true
3. Speak kind-ly, speak kind-ly; kind words nev - er yet Brought ha - tred or

kindness are bet-ter than gold. { Kind words ev'ry morning, kind words ev'ry night, / And kind words for-ev -- er, in dark days or bright. }
kindness to cheer and to bless: { It soothes ev'ry sorrow, makes smooth ev'ry path; / It light - ens all burdens, and turns away wrath. }
dis - cord, or grief or re-gret. { Speak kindly, speak kindly and then nev - er fear: / Life's lil - ies and ros - es will bloom all the year. }

CHORUS. *Repeat Softly.*

Speak kindly, speak kindly to young and to old, The words of true kindness are better than gold.

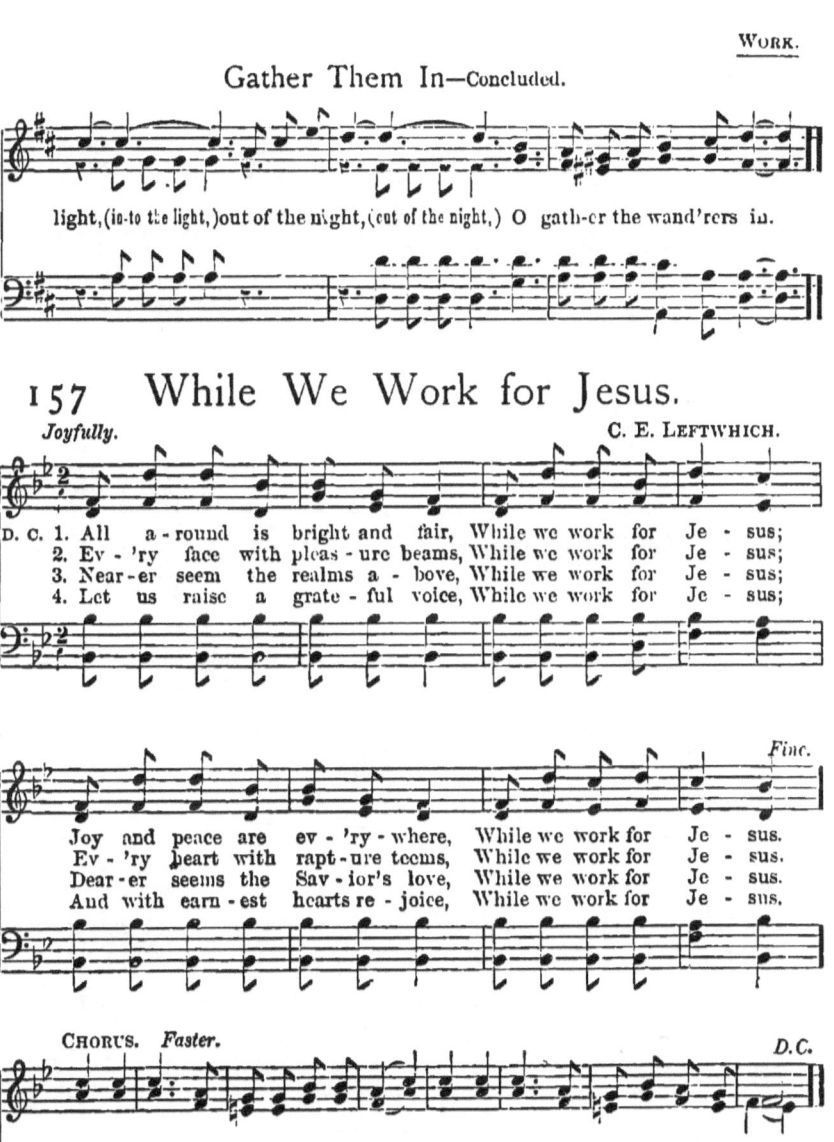

158. On the Jericho Road.

Dr. J. J. Maxfield. — W. A. Ogden.

1. On the Jer-i-cho road there is ser-vice to-day, For all who are ready to work or to pray; A-round us are ly-ing the wound-ed and dy-ing, And few the Sa-mar-i-tans pass-ing that way.
2. On the Jer-i-cho road you will find him to-day, Your broth-er who wan-ders from Je-sus a-way; Oh, wait not to-mor-row, his deep cup of sor-row Is brimming and bit-ter, no lon-ger de-lay.
3. On the Jer-i-cho road ma-ny for-ces com-bine, To sti-fle the voice of the Spir-it Di-vine; A-bout us are ly-ing the wound-ed and dy-ing, Go, broth-er, and pour in the oil and the wine.

Chorus.

On the Jer-i-cho road, leading down, down, down, down, The Le-vite goes carelessly by,

WORK.

On the Jericho Road.—Concluded.

Yet ma-ny who journey a-long that way, Are wound-ed and ready to die.

159 We Will Labor.

ALEX. THOMAS.   Arr. by S. W. S.

1. Je-sus needs the lit-tle chil-dren, He has work for each of you.
2. Oh, he loves the cheerful work-er, Who can bright-er make the way;
3. Lit-tle acts for Je-sus' glo-ry, Help to make a world of love,

In his wide and pleas-ant vine-yard, There are lov-ing tasks to do.
Com-fort-ing the sick and lone-ly; Light-ing up the drear-y day.
And to fit the lit-tle work-er, For a bet-ter home a-bove.

CHORUS.

{ We will la-bor in his vine-yard, Joy-ful-ly his bid-ding do; }
{ Ful-ly trust-ing in his prom-ise, For his prom-is-es are true. }

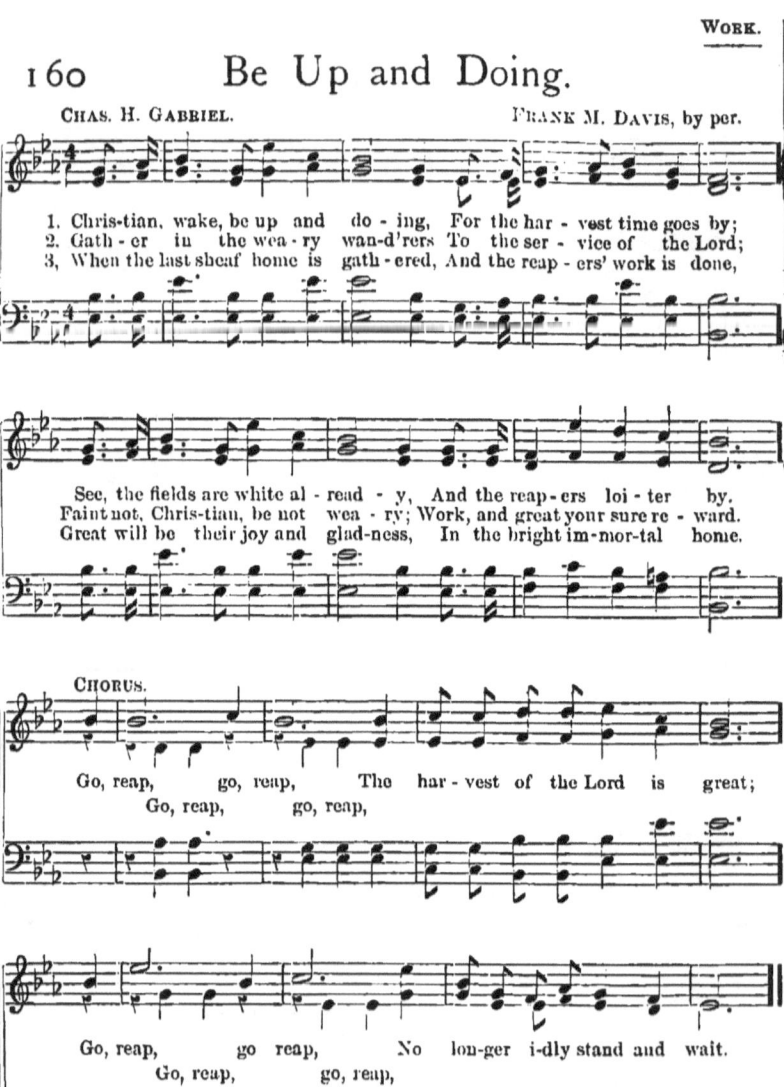

162 We should Hear the Angels Singing!

KATE CAMERON. S. W. STRAUB.

1. If we on - ly sought to bright-en Ev - 'ry path - way dark with care,
2. If we on - ly strove to cher - ish Ev - 'ry pure and ho - ly thought
3. If it were our aim to pon - der On the good that we might win,
4. If we on - ly did our du - ty, Think-ing not what it might cost

If we on - ly tried to light - en All the bur - dens oth-ers bear;
Till with-in our hearts should per-ish All that is with e - vil fraught
Soon our feet would cease to wan - der In for - bid - den paths of sin.
Then the earth would wear new beau-ty, Fair as that in E - den lost.

CHORUS.

We should hear the an - gels sing-ing, All a - round us, night and day;

We should feel that they are wing-ing, At our side, their up - ward way.

164 A Voice I Hear.

R. L. W. Arr. *Moderato.* R. L. W

1. There's a voice I hear, and it calls me u
2. There is *One* a-bove, look-ing down in lo
3. Oh, the bit-ter cries, and the long-ing ey

lov-ing side, And it says to me, "You
sunk in sin; And I hear him call, to
hear and see; For our love they plead, an

If you'll on-ly fol-low where I guide."
"Who will go and bring the lost ones in?"
Shall we sav-iors of the lost ones be?

stray from the Cross of Cal-va-ry,

INVITATION AND APPEAL

A Voice I Hear—Concluded.

ban-ner of the Son of God; There is pu-ri-ty and pow'r,
There is vic-t'ry ev-'ry hour, When we're liv-ing 'neath the smile of God.

165 Poor Sinner, Lov'st Thou Me?

WM. COWPER. *ab.*   J. B. DYKES.

1. Hark, my soul! it is the Lord, 'Tis thy Sav-ior, hear his word;
2. "I de-liv-ered thee when bound, And, when bleed-ing, healed thy wound;
3. "Mine is an un-chang-ing love, High-er than the heights a-bove,
4. "Thou shalt see my glo-ry soon, When the work of grace is done;
5. Lord, it is my chief com-plaint, That my love is weak and faint;

Je-sus speaks, and speaks to thee;   "Say, poor sin-ner, lov'st thou me?
Sought thee wandering, set thee right.   Turn'd thy dark-ness in-to light.
Deep-er than the depths be-neath,   Free and faith-ful, strong as death.
Part-ner of my throne shalt be: Say, poor sin-ner, lov'st thou me?"
Yet, I love thee and a-dore!   Oh, for grace to love thee more!

INVITATION AND APPEAL.

166 Hear the Precious Words of Life.

MARIA STRAUB.   S. W. STRAUB.

1. O hark - en to your Sav-ior, Friend, He'll guide you to the right, He'll lead you thro' the gloom-y way In - to the path of light; He is the teacher sent from heav'n In whom God is well pleased, Then hear ye him, ye err-ing ones, And be from sin re-leased.
2. He came to earth, the Prince of Peace, To tell of things a-bove: He comes to bring sal - va-tion near, To show a Fa-ther's love; O list - en to his glo-rious words, They bid the dark-ness fly, They still the tem-pest, calm the sea, And bring sweet comfort nigh.
3. From heav'n still comes that gen - tle voice, It comes to us to - day, Say-ing, "Tis my be - lov - ed Son; Then hear him and o - bey." He who would reach that bet - ter land Where shad-ows nev-er dim, Must fol-low the good Shep-herd's call, Then, pil-grims, "Hear ye him."

CHORUS. Je-sus says his words are life,—Hear ye Hear ye him, O

INVITATION AND APPEAL.

Hear the Precious Words of Life—Concluded.

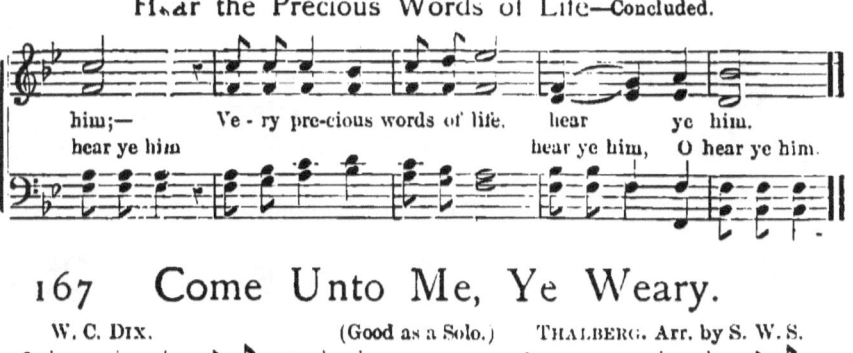

him;— Ve - ry pre-cious words of life. hear ye him.
hear ye him hear ye him, O hear ye him.

167 Come Unto Me, Ye Weary.

W. C. DIX. (Good as a Solo.) THALBERG. Arr. by S. W. S.

1. "Come un - to me, ye wea-ry, And I will give you rest." O bless-ed voice of
2. "Come un - to me, ye fainting, And I will give you light;" O lov - ing voice of
3. "Come un - to me, ye wea-ry, And I will give you life." O cheer-ing voice of
4. "And who - so ev - er com-eth, I will not cast him out;" O wel-come voice of

Je - sus, Which comes to hearts op press'd: It tells of ben - e - dic-tion, Of
Je - sus, Which comes to cheer the night; Our hearts were filled with sad-ness, And
Je - sus, Which comes to aid our strife; The foe is stern and ea - ger, The
Je - sus, Which drives a-way our doubt; Which calls us, ver - y sin-ners, Un-

rit.

par-don, grace, and peace, Of joy that hath no end-ing, Of love that cannot cease.
we had lost our way; But he has bro't us gladness And songs at break of day.
fight is fierce and long; But he has made us mighty, And stronger than the strong.
worth-y tho' we be Of love so free and boundless, To come, dear Lord, to thee.

INVITATION AND APPEAL.

The Spirit and the Bride Say, Come—Concluded.

Come, says the Spir-it, Come, says the Bride; Who-so ev-er will may come.

Mornington.

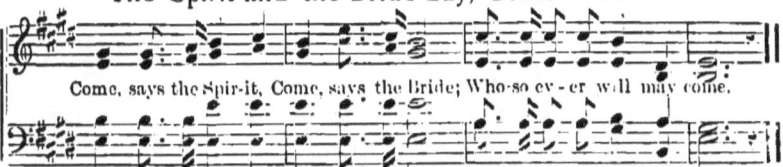

171

1 The Spirit, in our hearts,
  Is whispering, "Sinner, come!"
  The Bride, the Church of Christ, pro-
  To all his Children, "Come!" [claims

2 Let him that heareth say
  To all about him, "Come!"
  Let him that thirsts for righteousness,
  To Christ, the Fountain, come!

3 Yes, whosoever will,
  O, let him freely come,
  And freely drink the stream of life;
  'Tis Jesus bids him come.

172

1 Ye sons of earth, arise,
  Ye creatures of a day;
  Redeem the time—be bold—be wise,
  And cast your bonds away.

2 The year of gospel grace
  With us rejoice to see,
  And thankfully in Christ embrace
  Your proffered liberty.

3 Blest Savior, Lord of all,
  God help us to receive;
  Obedient to thy gracious call,
  O, bid us turn and live.

Peterborough.

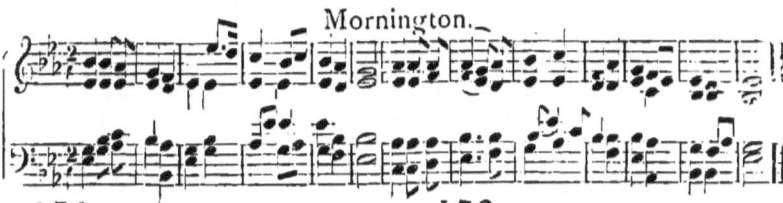

173

1 Let every mortal ear attend,
  And every heart rejoice;
  The trumpet of the gospel sounds
  With an inviting voice.

2 Eternal wisdom has prepared
  A soul-reviving feast,
  And bids your longing appetites
  The rich provision taste.

3 Ho! ye that pant for living streams,
  And pine away and die,— [thirst
  Here you may quench your raging
  With springs that never dry.

174

1 Return, O wanderer, now return,
  And seek thy Father's face;
  Those new desires, which in thee burn,
  Were kindled by his grace.

2 Return, O wanderer, now return;
  He hears thy humble sigh;
  He sees thy softened spirit mourn,
  When no one else is nigh.

3 Return, O wanderer, now return,
  And wipe the falling tear;
  Thy Father calls—No longer mourn;
  'Tis love invites thee near.

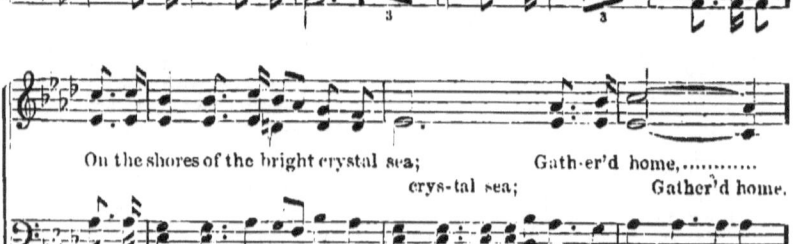

HEAVEN.

179 My Eternal Home.
BONAR. FLOTOW.

1. This is not my place of rest-ing, Mine's a cit-y yet to come;
2. In it all is light and glo-ry; O'er it shines a night-less day:
3. There the Lamb, our Shep-herd, leads us By the streams of life a - long;—

On - ward to it I am hast-ing On to my e - ter - nal home.
Ev - 'ry trace of sin's sad sto - ry, Gone for-ev - er, pass'd a - way.
On the fresh-est pas-tures feeds us, Turns our sigh-ing in - to song.

180 Heaven is Our Home.
T. R. TAYLOR. ARTHUR SULLIVAN.

1. We are but stran-gers here, Heav'n is our home; Earth is a
2. What tho' the tem-pests rage? Heav'n is our home; Short is our
3. There at our Sav-ior's side, Heav'n is our home; May we be

des-ert drear, Heav'n is our home; Dan-ger and sor-row stand Round us on
pil-grim-age, Heav'n is our home; And time's wild wintry blast Soon shall be
glor - i - fied, Heav'n is our home. There are the good and blest, Those we love

Heaven is Our Home—Concluded.

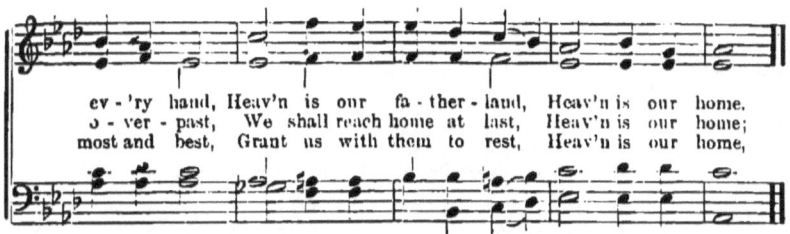

181 The Glorious World on High

ZEUNER.

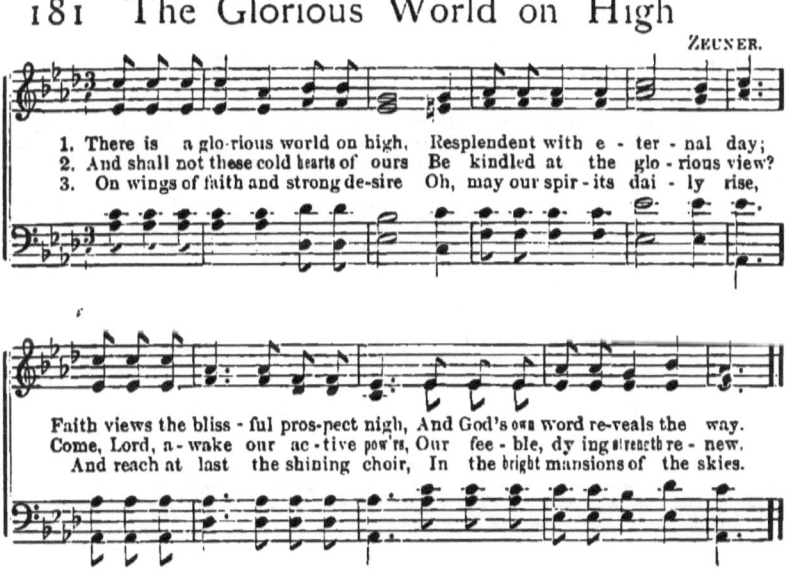

1. There is a glorious world on high, Resplendent with eternal day;
2. And shall not these cold hearts of ours Be kindled at the glorious view?
3. On wings of faith and strong desire Oh, may our spirits daily rise,

Faith views the bliss-ful prospect nigh, And God's own word reveals the way.
Come, Lord, awake our active pow'rs, Our feeble, dying strength renew.
And reach at last the shining choir, In the bright mansions of the skies.

182

1 There is a world we have not seen,
   That wasting time can ne'er destroy,
   Where mortal footsteps have not been,
   Nor ear hath caught its sounds of joy.

2 It is not fanned by summer gale;
   'Tis not refreshed by vernal showers,

   It never needs the moonbeam pale.
   For there are known no evening hours.

3 There forms unseen by mortal eye,
   Too glorious for our sight to bear,
   Are walking with their God on high,
   And waiting our arrival there.

184. I Love Thy Church.

FELLOWSHIP.
A. WILLIAMS

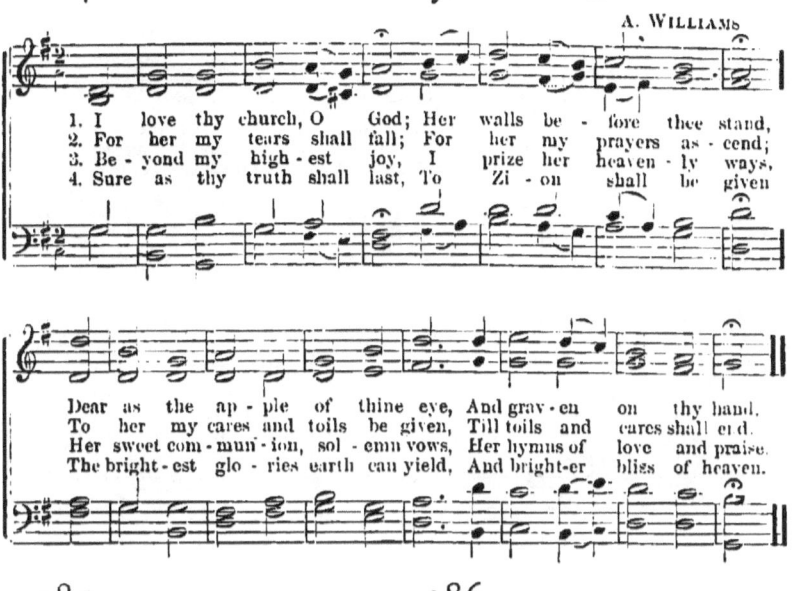

1. I love thy church, O God; Her walls before thee stand,
Dear as the apple of thine eye, And graven on thy hand.

2. For her my tears shall fall; For her my prayers ascend;
To her my cares and toils be given, Till toils and cares shall end.

3. Beyond my highest joy, I prize her heavenly ways,
Her sweet communion, solemn vows, Her hymns of love and praise.

4. Sure as thy truth shall last, To Zion shall be given
The brightest glories earth can yield, And brighter bliss of heaven.

185

(The above Tune, or Dennis, key of F.)

1 Blest be the tie that binds
Our hearts in Christian love;
The fellowship of kindred minds
Is like to that above.

Before our Father's throne
We pour our ardent prayers;
Our fears, our hopes, our aims are one,
Our comforts and our cares.

3 We share our mutual woes,
Our mutual burdens bear;
And often for each other flows
The sympathizing tear.

4 When we asunder part,
It gives us inward pain;
But we shall still be joined in heart,
And hope to meet again.

5 This glorious hope revives
Our courage by the way,
While each in expectation lives,
And longs to see the day.

186

1 Love is the strongest tie
That can our hearts unite,
Love makes our service liberty,
Our every burden light.

2 We run in God's commands,
When love directs the way;
With willing hearts and active hands,
Our Maker's will obey.

3 Love softens all our toil,
And makes our bondage blest;
The gloomy desert wears a smile,
When love inspires the breast.

4 Let love forever grow,
And banish wrath and strife;
So shall we witness here below,
The joys of social life.

5 When we ascend the skies,
And see the Savior's face,
Love will to full perfection rise,
And reign through all the place.

HEAVEN.

188 The Universal Song.
JOHN STAINER:

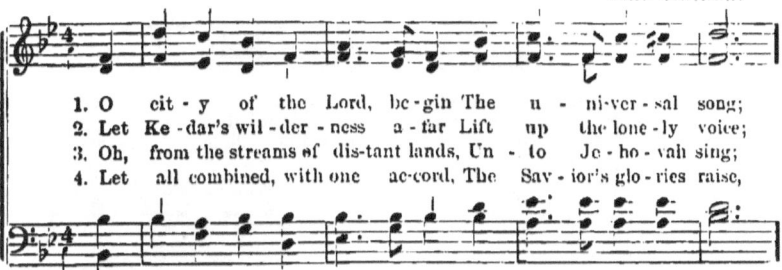

1. O cit-y of the Lord, be-gin The u-ni-ver-sal song;
2. Let Ke-dar's wil-der-ness a-far Lift up the lone-ly voice;
3. Oh, from the streams of dis-tant lands, Un-to Je-ho-vah sing;
4. Let all combined, with one ac-cord, The Sav-ior's glo-ries raise,

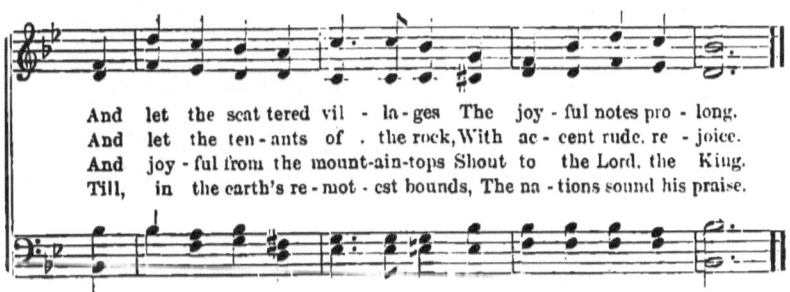

And let the scat tered vil-la-ges The joy-ful notes pro-long.
And let the ten-ants of the rock,With ac-cent rude, re-joice.
And joy-ful from the mount-ain-tops Shout to the Lord, the King.
Till, in the earth's re-mot-est bounds, The na-tions sound his praise.

189 Missionary Hymn.
Key of E.

1 Hail to the Lord's Anointed,
    Great David's greater Son!
Hail! in the time appointed
    His reign on earth begun!
He comes to break oppression,
    To set the captive free,
To take away transgression,
    And rule in equity.

2 He shall descend like showers
    Upon the fruitful earth,
And love and joy, like flowers,
    Spring in his path to birth;
Before him, on the mountains,
    Shall peace, the herald, go;
And righteousness, in fountains,
    From hill to valley flow.

190 Webb.
Key of B Flat.

1 The morning light is breaking,
    The darkness disappears:
The sons of earth are waking
    To penitential tears;
Each breeze that sweeps the ocean
    Brings tidings from afar
Of nations in commotion,
    Prepared for Zion's war.

2 Blest river of salvation.
    Pursue thy onward way;
Flow thou to every nation,
    Nor in thy richness stay;
Stay not till all the lowly
    Triumphant reach their home:
Stay not till all the holy
    Proclaim—"The Lord has come!

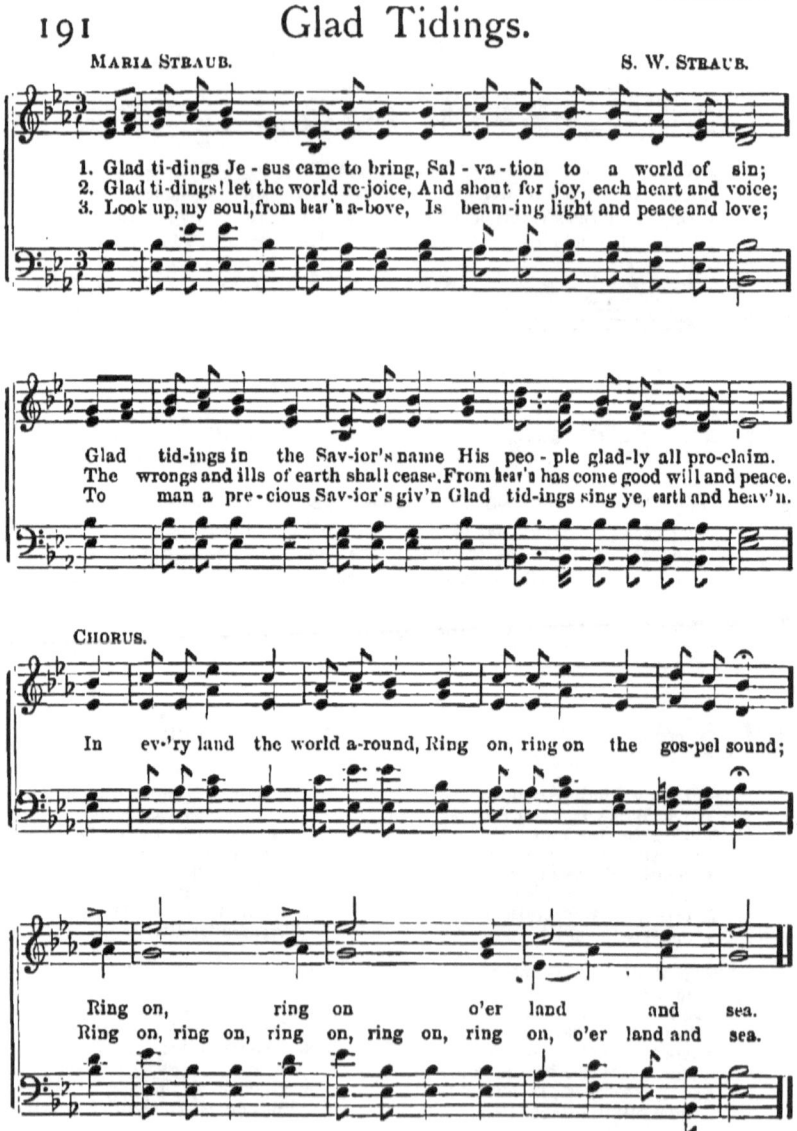

MISSIONARY

192. Jesus Shall Reign.

W. H. GLADSTONE.

1. Je-sus shall reign where'er the sun   Does his suc-ces-sive jour-neys run;
2. To him shall end-less pray'r be made, And end-less prais-es crown his head;
3. Peo-ple and realms of ev - 'ry tongue Dwell on his love, with sweetest song;
4. Let ev-'ry crea-ture rise and bring Pe-cu-liar hon - ors to our King:

His king-dom stretch from shore to shore, Till moons shall wax and wane no more.
His name, like sweet per-fume, shall rise With ev-'ry morn-ing sac - ri - fice.
And in-fant voic - es   shall pro-claim Their ear-ly bless-ings on his name.
An - gels de-scend with songs a - gain, And earth re-peat the loud A - men.

193

1 We long to see that happy time,
  That long-expected, blissful day,
  When men of every name and clime
  The glorious gospel shall obey.

2 The word of God shall firm abide, [pose;
  Though earth and hell should dare op-
  The stone cut from the mountain's side,
  To universal empire grows.

3 Afric's emancipated sons
    Shall shout to Asia's rapturous song,
  Europe, with her unumbered tongues
    And western climes the strain prolong,

194

(The above Tune, or Marlow, No. 27, key of G.)

1 Soon may the last glad song arise
  Through all the millions of the skies,
  That song of triumph which records
  That all the earth is now the Lord's!

2 Let thrones and powers and kingdoms be
    Obedient, mighty Lord, to thee!
  And over land, and stream and main,
    Wave thou the sceptre of thy reign!

3 Oh, let that glorious anthem swell,
  Let host to host the triumph tell
  That not one rebel heart remains,
  But over all the Savior reigns!

CHRISTMAS.

196   The Angels' Song.

M. S.   S. W. S.

1. Joy! joy! O hear the sound, Glad ti - dings an - gels bring;
2. Joy! joy! let all the world Re - joice, the Lord has come;
3. Joy! joy! the Lord has come! O wel - come Prince of peace: —

'Tis the time so long fore-told, The an - gels sweet-ly sing.
Wake! a - wake, each heart and voice, To sing the an - gels' song.
Na - tions now shall all be one, All strife and e - vil cease.

CHORUS.

Glo - ry to God in the high - est, Peace on earth, good will to men;

Glo - ry to God in the high - est, Peace on earth, good will to men.

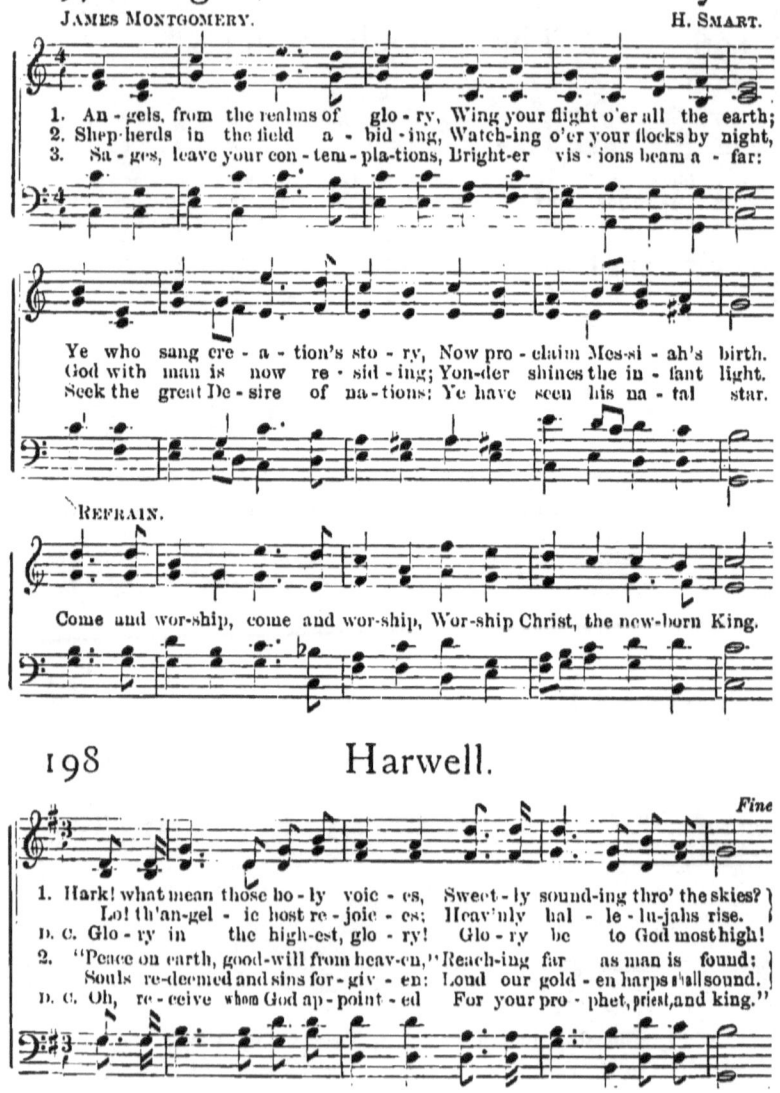

CHRISTMAS.

Harwell—Concluded.

List - en to the won-d'rous sto-ry Which they chant in hymns of joy;
Christ is born, the great a - noint-ed; Heav'n and earth his praises sing!

199 Glory to God.

MENDELSSOHN.

1. Hark! hark! with harps of gold, What an-them do they sing? The radiant clouds have
2. "Glo-ry to God!" re-peat The glad earth and the sea; And ev - 'ry wind and
3. Soft swells the mu-sic now A - long that shin-ing choir, And ev - 'ry ser - aph
4. Soft! yet the soul is bound With rap-ture like a chain: Earth, vo-cal, whispers

back-ward roll'd, And an-gels smite the string. "Glory to God!" bright wings Spread glist'ning
bil - low fleet bears on the ju - bi - lee. Where Hebrew bard hath sung, Or Hebrew
bends his brow And breathes above his lyre. What words of heav'nly birth Thrill deep our
them a-round, And heav'n repeats the strain. Sound, harps, and hail the morn With ev - 'ry

and a - far. And on the hal-low'd rap-ture rings From cir-cling star to star.
seer hath trod; Each ho - ly spot has found a tongue: "Let glo - ry be to God."
hearts a - gain, And fall like dew-drops to the earth? "Peace and good will to men!"
gold-en string; For un - to us this day is born A Sav - ior and a King!

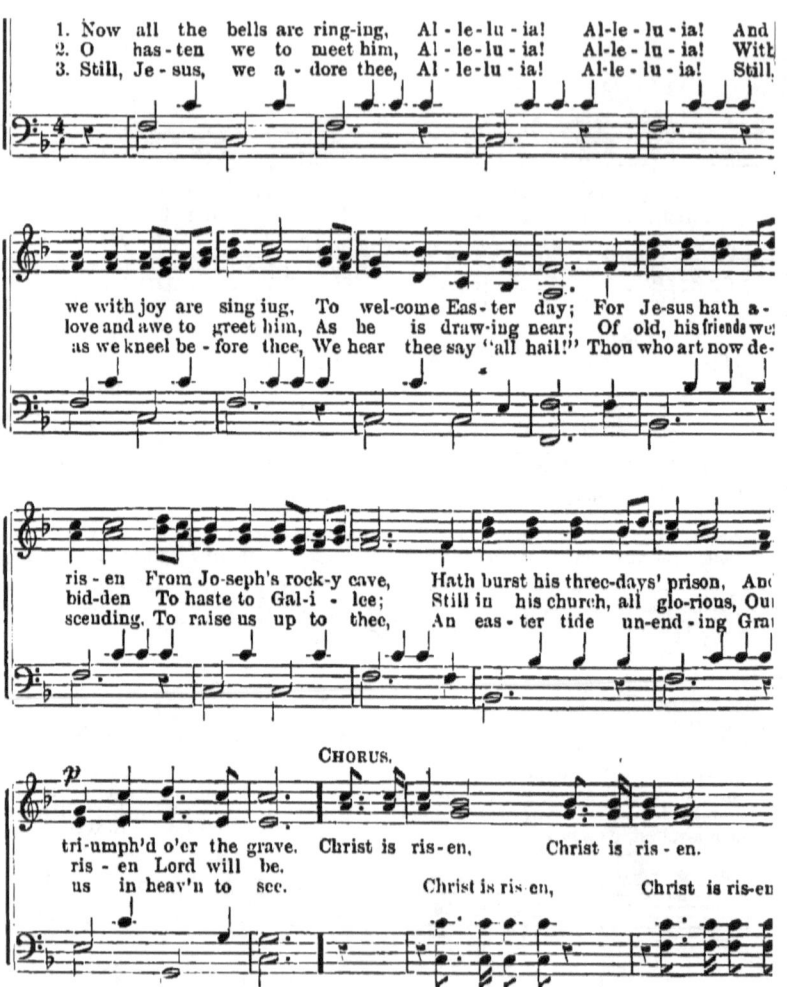

EASTER.

202. The Lord is Arisen.

Translated from the German by MARIA STRAUB. Arr. from German.

1. I love the bright spring-time, I love the fair bloom, No bird like the spring-bird my heart can at-tune; I think, as I list, of that other spring-time When wakened the heart to the heav-en-ly chime, "The Lord is a-ris-en and go-eth be-fore, Go tell his dis-ci-ples and sor-row no more," The Lord is a-true.

2. I love the bright spring-time of good tho't and deed, The wak-ing to life of the good sower's seed; I'm grate-ful for all the bright blooms of the spring, I remember my Sav-ior and glad-ly I sing, "The Lord is a-ris-en, the tid-ings are true. The Lord is a-ris-en, for me and for you, The Lord is a-

EASTER.

The Lord is Arisen—Concluded.

ris-en, O sing it glad heart, The Lord is a-ris-en, let sor-row de-part.
ris-en, O sing it glad heart, The Lord is a-ris-en, let sor-row de-part.

203 The Day of Resurrection.

Arr. from F. GUMBERT.

1. The Day of Res-ur-rec-tion! Earth, tell it out a-broad; The Pass-o-ver of
2. Our hearts be pure from e-vil, That we may see a-right The Lord in rays e-
3. Now let the heav'ns be joy-ful, And earth her song be-gin, The round world keep high

glad-ness, The Pass-o-ver of God; From death to life e-ter-nal, From
ter-nal Of res-ur-rec-tion-light; And, listening to his ac-cents, May
tri-umph, And all that is there-in: Let all things seen and un-seen Their

earth un-to the sky, Our Christ hath brought us o-ver, With hymns of vic-to-ry.
hear so calm and plain His own "All hail," and hearing May raise the vic-tor strain.
notes of gladness blend, For Christ the Lord is ris-en, Our joy that hath no end.

FUNERAL.

205 Our Treasures.

M. E. SERVOSS. S. W. STRAUB.

1. Gen - tly as the wind of au - tumn Car-ries far the tint - ed leaf,
2. As we weave the au - tumn treas-ures In - to wreaths of col - ors bright,
3. As we keep the rich - est leaf - lets, Till an-oth - er spring shall come,

So the an - gel reap - er, com - ing, Bore a - way our golden sheaf;
So the Mas - ter sets our jew - els In his hal-lowed crown of light;
So our Fa - ther keeps our dar-lings Till we reach our heav'n-ly home;

Up to the e - ter - nal sum - mer, To a land all bright and fair,
There they shine in won-drous beau - ty, Where no moth nor rust de - cay,
There with-in the gates so pearl - y, We shall find them hand in hand,

Where no storm-clouds ev - er gath - er We shall find it gar-ner'd there.
Treas-ures in our Fa - ther's kingdom Safe thro' all e - ter - ni - ty.
Wait-ing for us in the spring time, Of that oth - er, bet - ter land.

FUNERAL.

206 We Soon Shall Meet Above.

S. W. STRAUB.

1. How sweet to think when we are torn From those we fond-ly love;
2. When na-ture's strong, yet ten-der tie, By death are torn a-part;
3. When loved com-pan-ions, dear and true, The friends of hap-py years,

How sweet to think, when called to mourn, We soon shall meet a-bove.
This tho't the sooth-ing balm sup-plies That heals the wounded heart.
Must bid a long and last a-dieu, This tho't can dry their tears.

CHORUS.

We soon shall meet,............... shall meet a-bove..................
We soon shall meet, shall meet a-bove.

207 C. M.

1 Death is the fading of a cloud,
　The breaking of a chain;
　The rending of a mortal shroud
　We ne'er shall see again.

2 Death is the conqueror's welcome home,
　The heavenly city's door;
　The entrance of the world to come—
　'Tis life for evermore.

3 Death is the mightier second birth,
　Th' unvailing of the soul;
　'Tis freedom from the chains of earth,
　The pilgrim's heavenly goal.

4 Death is the close of life's alarms,
　The watch-light on the shore;
　The clasping in immortal arms
　Of loved ones gone before.

5 Death is the gaining of a crown
　Where saints and angels meet;
　The laying of our burden down
　At the Deliverer's feet.

6 Death is a song from seraph lips,
　The day-spring from on high;
　The ending of the soul's eclipse,—
　Its transit to the sky.

PATRIOTIC.

208. Our Country's Banner.

L. F. L.
L. F. LINDSAY.

1. This is our coun-try's cel - e - bra-tion, So ma - ny years has borne us on;
2. Colum-bia's hope is in her children, Its flag they'll bear thro' many a fight,
3. Then lift on high this glo-rious banner, Our country's God, to thee we sing;

Freedom and God were its sal - va-tion, Its rock was right, by this it won.
Till ev - 'ry na - tion learns its freedom, And serves our God with freedom's light.
Let its bright folds pro-tect us ev - er, And cov'r it with thy shelt'ring wing.

CHORUS.

Hur-rah! hur-rah! for our country's banner, Let its bright folds re-main un-furl'd,

Till ev - 'ry na-tion learns the ti-dings, Freedom and truth for all the world.

PATRIOTIC.

209 America.

SAMUEL J. SMITH.

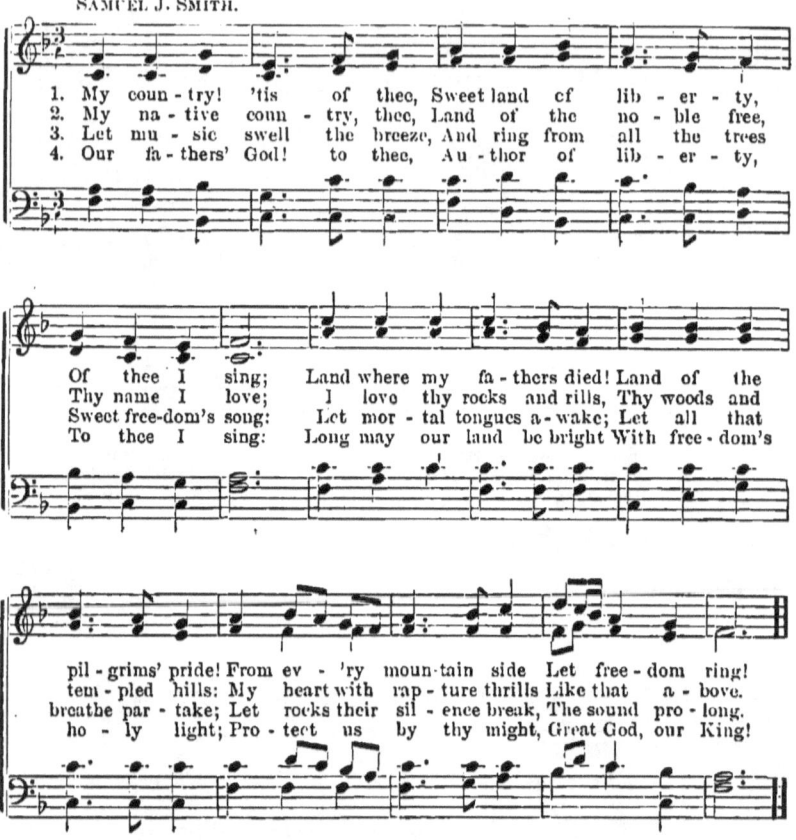

1. My coun-try! 'tis of thee, Sweet land of lib-er-ty, Of thee I sing; Land where my fa-thers died! Land of the pil-grims' pride! From ev-'ry moun-tain side Let free-dom ring!
2. My na-tive coun-try, thee, Land of the no-ble free, Thy name I love; I love thy rocks and rills, Thy woods and tem-pled hills: My heart with rap-ture thrills Like that a-bove.
3. Let mu-sic swell the breeze, And ring from all the trees Sweet free-dom's song: Let mor-tal tongues a-wake; Let all that breathe par-take; Let rocks their si-lence break, The sound pro-long.
4. Our fa-thers' God! to thee, Au-thor of lib-er-ty, To thee I sing: Long may our land be bright With free-dom's ho-ly light; Pro-tect us by thy might, Great God, our King!

210

1 Great God of nations! now to thee
Our hymns of gratitude we raise:
With humble heart and bending knee
We offer thee our song of praise.

2 Here freedom spreads her banner wide,
And casts her soft and hallowed ray;
Here thou our fathers' steps did guide
In safety through their dangerous way.

3 We praise thee that the gospel's light
Through all our land its radiance sheds,
Dispels the shades of error's night,
And heavenly blessings round us spreads.

4 Great God! preserve us in thy fear;
In dangers still our guardian be;
O spread thy truth's bright precepts here,
Let all the people worship thee.

FLOWER SUNDAY.

211 For Me are all Life's Blessings.

MARIA STRAUB.   S. W. STRAUB.

1. For me the flow'rs are bloom-ing, So sweet-ly, bright-ly and gay,
2. For me are people so lov - ing, My fa - ther, moth-er, so dear;
3. For me are all of the good things, That tru - est friendship can give;

For me the song-birds are sing-ing, So cheer-i - ly through the day.
For me are words told so gen - tly That ev - er-y - where I hear.
For me are all of the bless-ings That free - ly let me live.

CHORUS.

For me, for me, is all the good I find,
For me, for me, is all the good I find,

And I, and I will love the Giv - er Kind.
And I, and I will love the Giv - er Kind.

CHILDREN'S DAY.

213. Beautiful Flowers.

M. A. S. *Sprightly*   ARTHUR M. STRAUB.

1. Oh, beau - ti-ful, beau - ti - ful flow - ers, They're bloom-ing for you and for me;
2. They tell of God's wis-dom and good - ness, In pal - ace or low cot-tage home;
3. They twine round the heart of af - fec - tion, They gar-land the brow of the fair:

They're an-gels of God by the way - side; His love in their fac - es I see.
They car - ry a mes-sage of kind-ness, Wher-ev - er their pres-ence is known.
They tell of a heav - en-ly Fa - ther, His won-der - ful love and care.

CHORUS.

Oh, flow - ers, beau - ti - ful flow - ers, So fresh, so fra - grant and fair;
They tell a sto - ry of glad - ness, They tell it ev - 'ry - where.

TEMPERANCE.

215 Rallying Song.

EMILY HUNTINGTON MILLER. GEO. F. ROOT.

1. Come, brave little soldiers, who stand for the right, Whose hearts they are val-iant and true;
2. There's ma-ny a tempt-er to lure you a-stray, For-get-ting your leader's command;
3. There's ma-ny a dan-ger, if i-dly you sleep, Forget-ting the e-vil to face;

There's ma-ny a bat-tle for he-roes to fight, But vic-t'ry is wait-ing for you.
No mat-ter how sweetly they call you a-way, Be sure that a foe is at hand.
But nothing can harm you, if bold-ly you keep Your watch as you stand in your place.

CHORUS.

For truth o-ver false-hood pre-vails, And wrong shall be van-quish'd by right;
And the Good and the True, and the Beautiful too, Shall conquer the world by their might.

Copyright, 1885, by Woman's Temp. Pub. Ass'n.

TEMPARANCE.

216. Temperance Battle Call.

ELLA J. BRUMBAUGH.   WM. BEERY.

1. A-wake! a-wake! gird on your ar-mor, Christ the Lord and Mas-ter calls;
2. A-rise and give your-self un-to Him, He hath done so much for you;
3. The Lord of hosts will sure-ly con-quer, He is stron-ger than the foe;

He bids you come and join the con-flict For the glo-rious Temp'rance cause.
En-list to-day a faith-ful sol-dier, Serv-ing all the jour-ney through.
And while He leads with sweet as-sur-ance, We may ev-er for-ward go.

CHORUS.

On! for the vic-to-ry is your re-ward, See the might-y tor-rent yields;
The peo-ple are cap-tive ta-ken for the Lord, He the scep-ter wields.

INFANT CLASS.

218   The Stars.

HAVERGAL.   RANDEGGER. Arr. by S. W. S.

1. The gold-en glow is pal-ing, Be-tween the cloud-y bars;
2. Are they the eyes of an - gels, That al-ways wake to keep
3. We hard-ly see them twink - le, In an - y sum-mer night,
4. More beau-ti-ful and glo-rious, And nev-er cold and far,

I'm watch-ing in the twi - light: To see the lit-tle stars.
A lov-ing watch a-bove us, While we are fast a-sleep?
But in the win-ter eve-nings The spark-le clear and bright;
Is he who al-ways loves them, The Bright and Morn-ing Star;

I wish that they would sing to-night, Their song of long a-go;
Or are they lamps that God has lit From his own glo-rious light,
Is this to tell the lit-tle ones, So hun-gry, cold and sad,
I wish those lit-tle chil-dren knew That ho-ly, hap-py light,

If we were on-ly near-er them, What might we hear and know!
To guide the lit-tle chil-dren's souls Whom he will call to-night.
That there's a shin-ing home for them, Where all is warm and glad?
Lord Je-sus, shine on them, I pray, And make them glad to-night

INFANT CLASS

220 Father, We Thank Thee.

S. W. STRAUB.

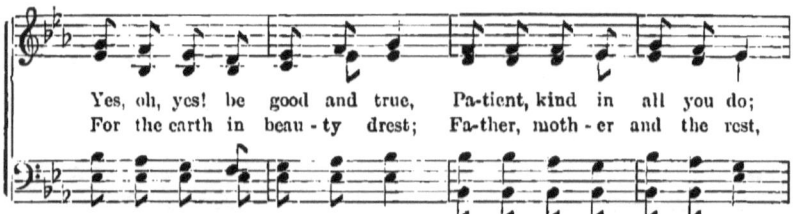

1. Can a lit-tle child like me Thank the Fa-ther fit-ting-ly?
2. For the fruit up - on the tree, For the birds that sing of thee!

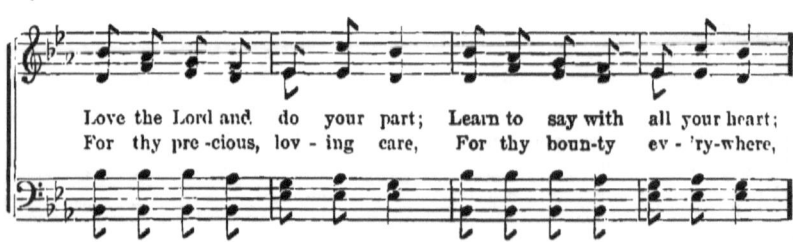

Yes, oh, yes! be good and true, Pa-tient, kind in all you do;
For the earth in beau-ty drest; Fa-ther, moth-er and the rest,

Love the Lord and do your part; Learn to say with all your heart;
For thy pre-cious, lov-ing care, For thy boun-ty ev-'ry-where,

CHORUS.

Fa-ther, we thank thee, Father, we thank thee, Fa-ther in heav-en, we thank thee!

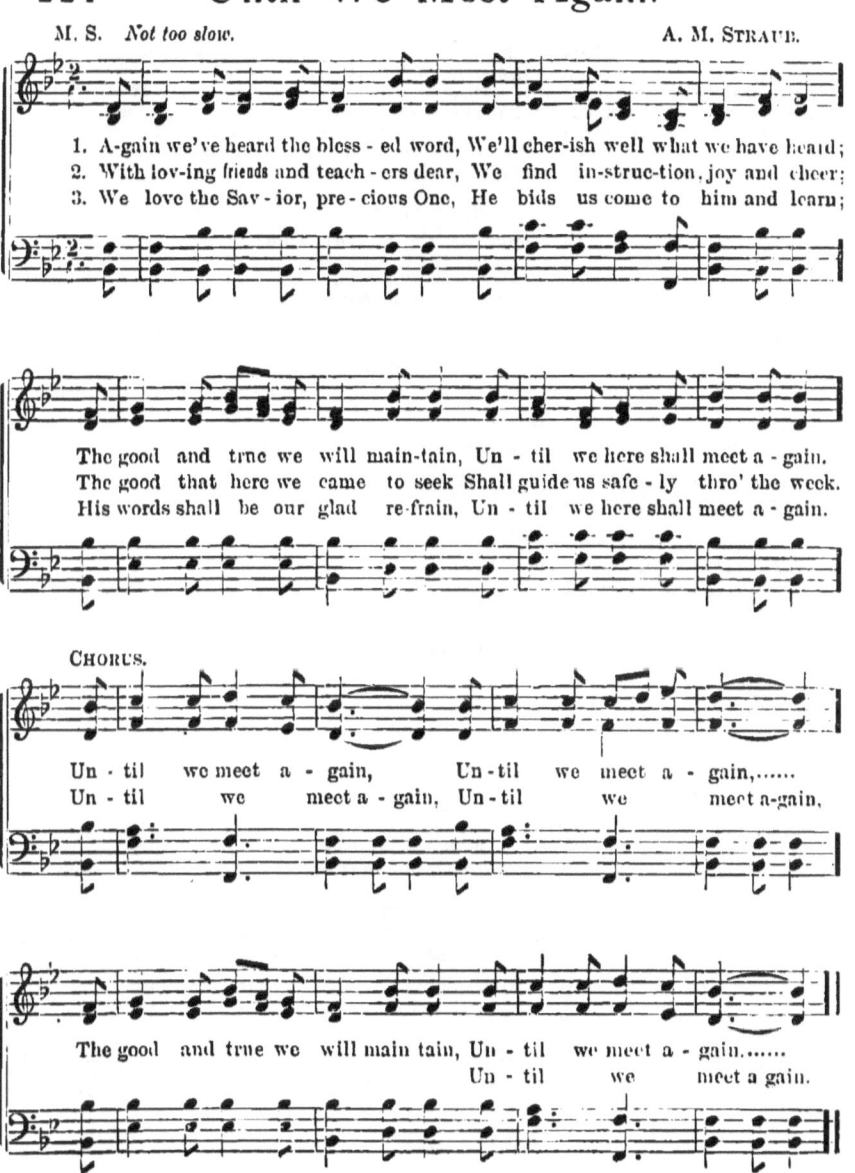

OPENING SERVICE.

222   God in his Works.

LEADER:
When I consider thy heavens, the work of thy fingers, the moon and the stars, which thou has ordained; what is man that thou art mindful of him? and the son of man, that thou visitest him?

For thou hast made him a little lower than the angels and hast crowned him with glory and honour.

O Lord, how manifold are thy works! in wisdom hast thou made them all. The earth is full of thy riches.

Who laid the foundations of the earth that it should not be removed forever.

The glory of the Lord shall endure forever: the Lord shall rejoice in his works.

(L. M. No. 150.)

The heavens declare thy glory, Lord,
In every star thy wisdom shines;
But when our eyes behold thy word
We read thy name in fairer lines.

Leader.—Bless the Lord, O my soul. O Lord my God, thou art very great.

Response.—Thou art clothed with honor and majesty;

L.—Thou visitest the earth, and waterest it: thou greatly enrichest it with the river of God, which is full of water.

R.—Thou makest it soft with showers: thou blessest the springing thereof.

L.—Thou crownest the year with goodness;

R.—And thy paths drop fatness.

L.—He watereth the hills from his chambers.

R.—The earth is satisfied with the fruit of thy works.

L.—He causeth the grass to grow for the cattle, and herb for service of man:

R.—That he may bring forth food out of the earth.

L.—The Lord hath prepared his throne in the heavens;

R.—And his kingdom ruleth over all.

PRAYER.

O thou Creator of all; maker of the heavens and the earth, we thank thee that thou art mindful of us, in preserving our lives and supplying our wants. O make us to realize more and more, that it is in thee that we live, move, and have our being. Thus shall we feel our dependence upon thee and learn the debt we owe thee. Help us O God to love thee supremely and our neighbor as ourselves, as thou lovingly requirest us. May we go about doing good in thy name, blessed Savior; and to thee be all the glory. Amen.

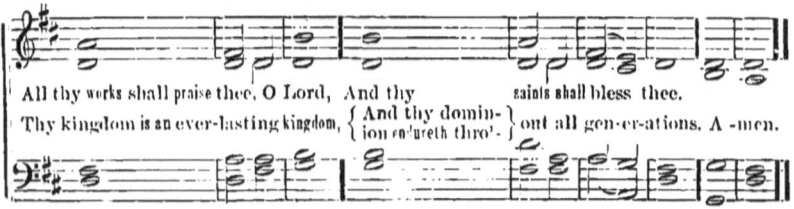

All thy works shall praise thee, O Lord, And thy saints shall bless thee.
Thy kingdom is an ever-lasting kingdom, { And thy domin- } out all gen-er-ations. A-men.
{ ion en-dureth thro'- }

223 Faith.

LEADER:
Therefore, being justified by faith, we have peace with God, through our Lord Jesus Christ.
By whom also we have access by faith into this grace wherein we stand, and rejoice in hope of the glory of God.

For ye are all children of God by faith in Christ Jesus.
Blessed are they that have not seen and yet have believed.
Watch ye, stand fast in the faith, quit you like men, be strong.

(Portuguese Hymn. Key of A, No. 117.)

How firm a foundation, ye saints of the Lord,
Is laid for your faith in his excellent word!
What more could he say than to you he hath said,
To you who for refuge to Jesus have fled?

"Fear not, I am with thee, O be not dismayed,
For I am thy God, I will still give thee aid:
I'll strengthen thee, help thee, and cause thee to stand,
Upheld by my gracious, omnipotent hand."

Leader—The Lord is my shepherd;

Response—I shall not want.

L.—He maketh me to lie down in green pastures:

R.—He leadeth me beside the still waters.

L.—He restoreth my soul:

R.—He leadeth me in the paths of righteousness for his name's sake.

L.—Yea, though I walk through the valley of the shadow of death, I will fear no evil:

R.—For thou art with me; thy rod and thy staff they comfort me.

L.—Thou preparest a table before me in the presence of mine enemies:

R.—Thou anointest my head with oil; my cup runneth over.

L.—Surely goodness and mercy shall follow me all the days of my life: and I will dwell in the house of the Lord forever.

R.—Blessed be the Lord forevermore.

PRAYER.

O God, we come to thee as little children unto a loving Father. Thou hast given us a hope for things unseen. And, knowing that unto thee all things must come, we ask that our hope, faith, and love may be strengthened and enlarged. So, that when our hearts are heavy laden, and spirits cast down by sorrow, we may apprehend in this life, something of the glory and joy to come. In the name of Christ we ask these things, now and evermore. Amen.

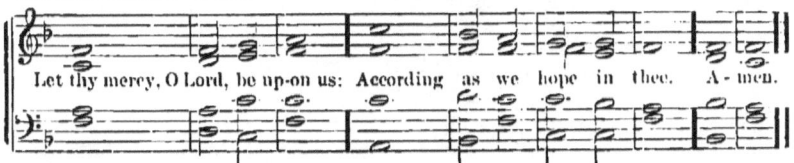

Let thy mercy, O Lord, be up-on us: According as we hope in thee. A-men.

OPENING SERVICE.

224   Praise to God.

LEADER:
Great is the Lord, and greatly to be praised; and his greatness is unsearchable.
The Lord is righteous in all his ways, and holy in all his works.
One generation shall praise thy works to another, and shall declare thy mighty acts.
They shall abundantly utter the memory of thy great goodness.
All thy works shall praise thee, O Lord; and thy saints shall bless thee.

Yea, happy is that people whose God is the Lord.
Thou openest thine hand, and satisfiest the desire of every living thing.
And in my prosperity I said, I shall never be moved.
Make a joyful noise unto the Lord, all ye lands.
Serve the Lord with gladness: come before his presence with singing.

(Duke St., L. M., No. 58, Key of E.)

O thou Creator, source of all,
Our hearts unite to sing thy praise;
Thy hand protects us through the night,
And yields the blessings of our days.

Leader.—Thou art my portion, O Lord; I have said that I would keep thy words.

Response.—Let thy mercies come also unto me, O Lord, even thy salvation.

L.—O satisfy us early with thy mercy;

R.—That we may rejoice and be glad all our days.

L.—O give thanks unto the Lord,

R.—For he is good; for his mercy endureth forever.

L.—O sing unto the Lord a new song:

R.—Sing unto the Lord all the earth.

L.—Give unto the Lord the glory due unto his name;

R.—Bring an offering, and come into his courts.

L.—My mouth shall speak the praises of the Lord:

All.—And let all flesh bless his holy name for ever and ever.

PRAYER.

Father in heaven, we thank thee for life and its joys, for the love of friends, for home and the fair world we live in, with its opportunities for making us thy good children. Our tongue shall praise thee for thy many good gifts bestowed upon us. May all learn to know thy love, that peace and joy may fill the whole earth; and to thee be honor and glory forever. Amen.

Oh, that men would praise the Lord for his goodness, And for his wonderful works to the children of men,
My mouth shall speak the praise of the Lord, { And all flesh shall bless his holy } name for-ever and ever, A - men.

225   God, the Father.

LEADER:
Have we not all one Father? Hath not one God created us? Why do we deal treacherously every man against his brother, by profaning the covenant of our fathers?

If ye had known me, ye should have known my Father also: and from henceforth ye know him, and have seen him.

Believe me that I am in the Father, and the Father in me: or else believe me for the very work's sake.

There is one body, and one Spirit, even as ye are called in one hope of your calling.

One God and Father of all, who is above all, and through all, and in you all.

(L. M. No. 93.)

What majesty and wondrous power,
Creator of the world is thine!
But O, thou art our Father too,
With love supreme, with love divine.

Leader.—Fear not, little flock;

Response.—For it is your Father's good pleasure to give you the kingdom.

L.—Lay up for yourselves treasures in heaven where neither moth nor rust doth corrupt, and where thieves do not break through nor steal.

R.—For the Lord is a God full of compassion and gracious, long-suffering, and plenteous in mercy.

L.—Be ye therefore merciful,

R.—As your Father also is merciful.

L.—Let your light so shine before men,

R.—That they may see your good works, and glorify your Father which is in heaven.

PRAYER.

Our Father which art in heaven, Hallowed be thy name. Thy kingdom come, thy will be done on earth as it is in heaven. Give us this day our daily bread, and forgive us our debts, as we forgive our debtors. And lead us not into temptation, but deliver us from evil: For thine is the kingdom, and the power, and the glory, forever. Amen.

Like as a father pitieth his children, So the Lord pit-ieth them that fear him. A-men.

OPENING SERVICE.

226   Christ the Teacher.

LEADER:
Take my yoke upon you, and learn of me; for I am meek, and lowly in heart: and ye shall find rest unto your souls.

For my yoke is easy, and my burden is light.

All things are delivered unto me of my Father: and no man knoweth the Son, but the Father; neither knoweth any man the Father, save the Son, and he to whomsoever the Son will reveal him.

I am the resurrection, and the life: he that believeth in me, though he were dead, yet shall he live.

Come unto me all ye that labor and are heavy laden, and I will give you rest.

(Missionary Hymn. L. M. Key of A flat. No. 181.)

Dear Lord, we come to learn of thee,
Nor fear to come, for thou art meek;
Thy love assures instruction free,
Thy wisdom, Lord, we gladly seek.

Leader.—And he opened his mouth, and taught them, saying,

Response.—Blessed are the poor in spirit: for theirs is the kingdom of Heaven.

L.—Blessed are they that mourn:

R.—For they shall be comforted.

L.—Blessed are the meek:

R.—For they shall inherit the earth.

L.—Blessed are they which do hunger and thirst after righteousness:

R.—For they shall be filled.

L.—Blessed are the merciful:

R.—For they shall obtain mercy.

L.—Blessed are the pure in heart:

R.—For they shall see God.

L.—Blessed are they which are persecuted for righteousness' sake:

R.—For theirs is the kingdom of heaven.

PRAYER.

Father in heaven, giver of every good and perfect gift, we thank thee for the gift of thy Son. We bless thy name for this great bounty, in sending him for our instruction and salvation. May we humbly and lovingly accept him as our teacher and Savior, follow in his footsteps in helping others into the way of life, and honoring and glorifying thy name on the earth. Dear Lord and Savior, we thank thee that thou hast promised to be with us even unto the end; thus shall we be comforted and strengthened when clouds come over our pathway. Grant us thy peace and blessing evermore. Amen.

'Teach me thy way O Lord; I will walk in thy truth, Unite my heart to fear thy name. A-men.

OPENING SERVICE.

227 Charity.

LEADER:
Though I speak with the tongues of men and angels, and have not charity, I am become as sounding brass, or a tinkling cymbal.
And though I have the gift of prophesy, and understand all mysteries and all knowledge; and though I have all faith, so that I could remove mountains, and have not charity, I am nothing.

And though I bestow all my goods to feed the poor, and though I give my body to be burned, and have not charity, it profiteth me nothing.
Charity never faileth: but whether there be prophesies, they shall fail; whether there be tongues, they shall cease; whether there be knowledge it shall vanish away.

(Balerma. C. M. Key of A.)

Come Holy Spirit, heavenly Dove,
With all thy quickening powers,
Kindle a flame of sacred love
In these cold hearts of ours.

Leader.—Love suffereth long,

Response.—And is kind;

L.—Love vaunteth not itself,

R.—Is not puffed up,

L.—Doth not behave itself unseemly,

R.—Seeketh not its own,

L.—Is not provoked,

R.—Taketh not account of evil;

L.—Rejoiceth not in unrighteousness,

R.—But rejoiceth with the truth;

L.—Beareth all things, believeth all things,

R.—Hopeth all things, endureth all things.

L.—But now abideth faith, hope, love, these three;

R.—And the greatest of these is love.

PRAYER.

Great God, our Creator and Preserver, we hallow thy name for it is love. We pray that the spirit of true love may live in our hearts, and find expression in our lives. Let thy compassion soften our hearts, and bind us in sympathy to kindred natures. O help us, that we may love thee supremely and our neighbor as ourselves. May we show this in deeds of kindness and the appreciation of thy goodness. And to thee shall be all the glory forever. Amen.

This is my com-mandment, That ye love one another as I have lov-ed you. A-men.

228 Christ the Example.

LEADER:
Then Jesus said unto his disciples, If any man will come after me, let him deny himself, and take up his cross and follow me.
For whosoever will save his life shall lose it: and whosoever will lose his life for my sake, shall find it.

Ye call me Master, and Lord: and ye say well: for so I am.
If I then your Lord and Master, have washed your feet, ye also ought to wash one another's feet.
For I have given you an example, that ye should do as I have done to you.
If ye know these things, happy are ye if ye do them.

(Pleyel's Hymn. 7s. Key of G.)

More like Jesus I would be,
Clothed with immortality,
Thinking not myself to please,
In the flow'ry beds of ease.

Leader.—What doth the Lord require of thee?

Response.—To do justly, to love mercy, and to walk humbly with our God.

L.—Blessed are the undefiled in the way,

R.—Who walk in the law of the Lord.

L.—Blessed are those servants whom the Lord shall find watching when he cometh;

R.—They shall receive the crown of life which the Lord hath promised to them that love him.

L.—Lead us, O Lord, in thy righteousness.

R.—Blessed is the man whom thou choosest, and causest to approach unto thee, that he may dwell in thy courts.

L.—Herein is my Father glorified, that ye bear much fruit

R.—So shall ye be my disciples.

L.—As the Father hath loved me so have I loved you:

R.—Continue ye in my love.

PRAYER.

Kind Father, we thank and adore thee for the many blessings bestowed upon us from day to day, and especially for thy kindly ministrations in sending thy Son, in whom thou art well pleased, to be the exemplar and guide through the shifting scenes of earth life. We thank thee that thou hast commanded us to hear him whose words are life and truth. O thou who art the life, the light, the truth, the way; help us to truly accept thee as our guide and ever seek to honor and glorify thee. Amen.

Christ also suffer'd for us, { Leaving us an example, that ye should } fol - low in his footsteps. A-men.

229   Forgiveness.

LEADER:
Woe unto you, when all men shall speak well of you! for so did their fathers to the false prophets.
But I say unto you which hear, Love your enemies, do good to them which hate you.
Bless them that curse you, and pray for them which despitefully use you.

And as ye would that men should do to you, do ye also to them likewise.
In honor preferring one another.
And be ye kind one toward another, tender hearted, forgiving one another, even as God for Christ's sake hath forgiven you.
Submitting yourselves one to another in the fear of God.

(Mornington. S. M. Key of E flat, No. 171.)

Lord such forgiving power,
As thine I fain would know ;
That, too, like thee, when foes assail,
I may forgiveness show.

Leader.—For if ye forgive men their trespasses, your heavenly Father will also forgive you.

Response.—But if ye forgive not men their trespasses, neither will your Father forgive your trespasses.

L.—The sacrifices of God are a broken spirit :

R.—A broken and a contrite heart, O God, thou wilt not despise.

L.—Hide thy face from my sins,

R.—And blot out all mine iniquities.

L.—Create in me a clean heart, O God ;

R.—And renew a right spirit within me.

L.—Cast me not away from thy presence ;

R.—And take not thy Holy Spirit from me.

L.—Let the wicked forsake his way, and the unrighteous man his thoughts: and let him return unto the Lord, and he will have mercy upon him ;

R.—And to our God, for he will abundantly pardon.

PRAYER.

Gracious Father, we come thanking thee for thy mercies manifest toward us. Knowing thy forgiving spirit we approach thee with confidence. Remembering that we are weak and erring creatures of thy hand, we can but trust thee to pardon all our shortcomings. O our Father, fill us with new desires for the good, and strengthen our feeble endeavors for the right. May thy love constrain us ever to keep in the path thou wouldst have us go. We ask it in the name of Jesus, our Lord. Amen.

Thou, Lord, art good and ready to for-give, And plenteous in mercy unto all them that call up-on thee. A-men.

230 Duty.

LEADER. Of his own will begat he us with the word of truth, that we should be a kind of first fruits of his creatures.

Wherefore, my beloved brethren, let every man be swift to hear, slow to speak, slow to wrath:

But be ye doers of the word, and not hearers only, deceiving your own selves. Therefore, to him that knoweth to do good, and doeth it not, to him it is sin.

(Webb. Key of B flat.)

Go forward, Christian soldier,
  Nor dream of peaceful rest,
'Till Satan's host is vanquished
  And heaven is all possest;
'Till Christ himself shall call thee
  To lay thine armor by,
And wear in endless glory,
  The crown of victory.

Leader.—The first of all the commandments is, Hear, O Israel;

Response.—The Lord our God is one Lord: And thou shalt love the Lord thy God with all thy heart, and with all thy soul, and with all thy mind, and with all thy strength.

L.—And the second is like, namely this:

R.—Thou shalt love thy neighbor as thyself.

L.—Bless the Lord, O my soul, and forget not all his benefits:

R.—Who forgiveth all thine iniquities; who healeth all thy diseases.

L.—Behold the eye of the Lord is upon them that fear him, upon them that hope in his mercy.

R.—God is greatly to be feared in the assembly of the saints, and to be had in reverence of all men that are about him.

L.—Our soul waiteth for the Lord;

R.—He is our help and our shield.

PRAYER.

Our Father, we find within our hearts the word which teaches us the way of life. Thou knowest our temptations, and because we sin we ask that the path of duty may be made plain. That our lives may be sweetened by the knowledge that thou wilt reveal, at last, unto all thy children, the beauties and wonders of thy love. May we become consecrated to thy will; and, through Christ, be led to serve Thee unto all the ages. Amen.

Let your light so shine before men, That they may see your good works and glorify your Father which is in heav'n. A-men.

OPENING SERVICE.

231 Christmas.

LEADER:
The people that walked in darkness have seen a great light; they that dwell in the land of the shadow of death, upon them hath the light shined.
For unto us a child is born, unto us a son is given, and the government shall be upon his shoulders; and his name shall be called Wonderful, Counsellor, The Mighty God, The Everlasting Father, The Prince of Peace.
Of the increase of his government and peace there shall be no end, upon the throne of David, and upon his kingdom, to order it, and to establish it with judgment and with justice, from henceforth even for ever.
The zeal of the Lord of hosts will perform this.

(Rockingham. L. M., No. 73.)

Hark! hark the sound, 'tis Christmas morn
The Savior, Prince of Peace is born!
Glory to God the angels sing,
Each heart receive your Lord and King.

Leader.—And there were in the same country shepherds abiding in the field,

Response.—Keeping watch over their flock by night.

L.—And, lo, the angel of the Lord came upon them, and the glory of the Lord shone round about them:

R.—And they were sore afraid.

L.—And the angel said unto them, Fear not:

R.—For, behold I bring you good tidings of great joy, which shall be to all people.

L.—For unto you is born this day in the city of David

R.—A Saviour, which is Christ the Lord.

L.—And suddenly there was with the angel a multitude of the heavenly host, praising God and saying,

R.—Glory to God in the highest, and on earth peace, good will toward men

PRAYER.

We praise thee, O God, for the gift of thy well beloved son, thine anointed; and we pray that our hearts may be more deeply impressed with thy great love. Help us, O God, so to receive him into our hearts, that we may glorify thy name, and establish peace and good will among men. Dear Saviour, sanctify us by thy spirit; save us from all sin, and thine be the glory forevermore. Amen.

Arise! shine for thy light is come, And the glory of the Lord is risen above thee. A-men.

OPENING SERVICE.

232 Easter.

LEADER:

I am the resurrection and the life: he that believeth in me, though he were dead, yet shall he live.

And whosoever liveth and believeth in me shall never die.

If in this life only we have hope in Christ, we are of all men most miserable.

But now is Christ risen from the dead, and become the first fruits of them that slept.

For since by man came death, by man also came the resurrection of the dead.

For as in Adam all die, even so in Christ shall all be made alive.

(Marlow. C. M., No. 27, Key of G.)

Rejoice all hearts, the Lord is risen,
And scattered is death's gloom!
He lives, and we shall also live,
Beyond the dreary tomb.

Leader.—The first man is of the earth, earthy:

Response.—The second man is the Lord from heaven.

L.—And as we have borne the image of the earthy,

R.—We shall also bear the image of the heavenly.

L.—For one star differeth from another star in glory.

R.—So also is the resurrection of the dead.

L.—It is sown in corruption;

R.—It is raised in incorruption:

L.—It is sown in dishonor;

R.—It is raised in glory:

L.—It is sown in weakness;

R.—It is raised in power.

L.—O, death where is thy sting? O grave where is thy victory?

R.—The sting of death is sin; and the strength of sin is the law.

PRAYER.

Father, we thank thee for this another morning commemorating the resurrection of our blessed Lord and Master. May his love be especially manifest to us while we contemplate his goodness represented in his devotion to others. May we imitate him by good words and deeds, helping everywhere the needy and distressed. Saviour, we thank thee that thou hast brought life and immortality to light; and may thy good spirit continue with us from day to day, to guide us to thy honor and glory. Amen.

If ye then be risen with Christ, seek those things which are a-bove, Where Christ sitteth on the right hand of God. A-men.

233. Temperance.

LEADER:
Happy is he that condemneth not himself in that thing which he alloweth.
It is good neither to eat flesh, nor to drink wine, nor anything whereby thy brother stumbleth, or is offended, or is made weak.
We then that are strong, ought to bear the infirmities of the weak, and not to please ourselves.

Let every one of us please his neighbor for his good to edification.
Love worketh no ill to his neighbor: therefore love is the fulfilling of the law.
Let every soul be subject unto the higher powers. For there is no power but of God: the powers that be are ordained of God.
Let us walk honestly, as in the day; not in rioting and drunkenness.

(Arlington. C. M., Key of G.)

Dear Savior guard us ev'ry hour,
By thy protecting care,
And save us from the tempter's power
To ruin and ensnare.

Leader.—Wine is a mocker, and strong drink is raging;

Response.—And whosoever is deceived thereby is not wise.

L.—Who hath woe? Who hath sorrow? Who hath contentions? Who hath babbling? Who hath wounds without cause? Who hath redness of eyes?

R.—They that tarry long at the wine; they that go to seek mixed wine.

L.—Look not thou upon the wine when it is red, when it giveth his colour in the cup, when it moveth itself aright.

R.—At the last it biteth like a serpent, and stingeth like an adder.

L.—Be not amongst wine-bibbers; amongst riotous eaters of flesh:

R.—For the drunkard and the glutton shall come to poverty: and drowsiness shall clothe a man with rags.

L.—Hear thou my son and be wise, and guide thine heart in the way. The father of the righteous shall greatly rejoice.

R.—Watch and pray lest ye enter into temptation.

PRAYER.

Heavenly Father, how often do we go astray,—wander into forbidden paths. We ask thee to forgive us and keep us in the better way. O Father, thou knowest the temptations that so constantly beset us. Keep us beneath thy watchful care. We would trust in thee, believing in thy love and power to restrain us in the evil hour. We are weak and need thine aid. Our help is in thee. Make us firm to do the right. Grant us thy peace dear Lord, and save us. Amen.

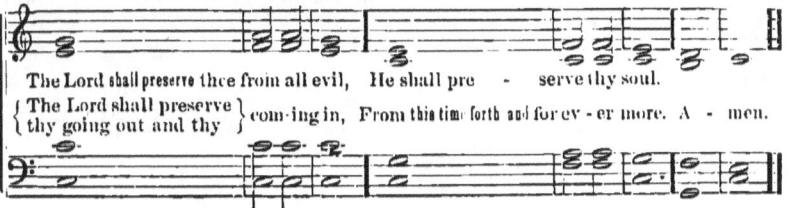

The Lord shall preserve thee from all evil, He shall pre - serve thy soul.
{ The Lord shall preserve thy going out and thy } com-ing in, From this time forth and for ev - er more. A - men.

INDEX.

Title in Capitals. First line in Roman.

ABIDE WITH ME................................. 33
Abide with me the Morning Sun 46
Again were heard the blessed word............221
A LAND OF PURE DELIGHT........ 175
All Around is Bright and Fair....................157
All Hail the Power of Jesus Name..... 169
ALL THINGS ARE OF GOD................. 72
ALL THINGS BEAUTIFUL................. 57
ALWAYS ABIDE WITH ME............ 46
ALWAYS SPEAK THE TRUTH.... 136
AMERICA..209
ANGELS FROM THE REALMS OF GLORY.197
ANGELS OF LIGHT........ ....1.6
Another Busy Week is Gone 6
Are You Building Your House on the Sand?...111
Are You Sowing the Seed of the Kingdom.....147
ARLINGTON..122
ASPIRATION... 31
A TRIBUTE BRING............. 9
A VOICE I HEAR 164
Awake! Awake, Gird on Your Arms...........216

BALERMA..121
BEAR YE ONE ANOTHER'S BURDENS....183
BEAUTIFUL FLOWERS 213
BE JOYFUL IN GOD................................. 1
BE NOT AFRAID..................................198
BETHANY... 34
Be the matter what it may................ 156
Be Thou, O God, Exalted High 7
BETTER HOPES 113
BETTER THAN GOLD.. 155
BE UP AND DOING.............................169
Blessed are the Pure in Heart..................106
Blessed Father with the Morning.............. 15
Blest be the Tie that Binds.....................185
BOYLSTON..140

Can You Count the Stars?........................ 56
Can a little child like me 220
CARRY US IN THINE ARMS............. 77
CHARITY (Opening Service)..................227
CHOOSE THOU FOR ME, MY GOD.........105
Christian, Wake, be Up and Doing 160
CHRIST IS RISEN................................200
CHRISTMAS (Opening Service)...............231
CHRIST THE EXAMPLE (Opening Service).224
CHRIST THE TEACHER (Opening Service) 226
Come Brave Little Soldiers...................215
COME, O CREATOR, SPIRIT BLEST........ 50
Come, Savior Jesus, from Above 95
Come thou Fount of Every Blessing 11
Come Thou Almighty King................... 4
Come to the Fountain 170
COME UNTO ME, YE WEARY.......... 167
CROWN HIM................................. ...201

Dear Jesus, be Thou Nigh Me.................. 45
Death is the Fading of a Flower 207
DESCEND UPON US........................... 54
DRINK AT THE FOUNTAIN................. 32
DUKE STREET................................ 58
DUTY (Opening Service)........................230

Earth with her Ten Thousand Flowers........ 61
EASTER (Opening Service)... 232

ETERNAL POWER..................................129
Eternal Power of Truth and Right.............129
Eternal Wisdom, Thee We Praise............... 28
EVENING SONG.... 18

FAITH (Opening Service) 223
Far from Mortal Cares Retreating 39
Father, Bend Thine Ear and Hear Me......... 41
Father, Forgive if Thy Goodness I Grieve....108
FATHER, HEAR ME..... 41
Father in Heaven, Thy Kingdom Come 35
FATHER, WE THANK THEE........ 231
Fear Not Sailor, Fear Not the Darkness.. ... 110
FORGIVENESS (Opening Service) 229
FOR ME ARE ALL LIFE'S BLESSINGS... 211
For Me the Flowers are Blooming 211
FORTH TO THE RESCUE GO...... 145
Forward be our Watchword................. . 127
FORWARD INTO LIGHT..... 127
From All Who Dwell in Heaven Above......... 58
FURTHER ON................................132

GATHERED HOME........................175
GATHER THEM IN 156
GENTLE SHEPHERD........................152
Gentle Shepherd, Gently Lead Us 42
Gentle as the Winds of Autumn 205
GIVE ME THE FAITH OF A CHILD.....108
Give to the Winds thy Fears... 140
GIVE US ENDURING FAITH.............104
GLAD TIDINGS.................................191
Glad Tidings Jesus Came to Bring 191
GLORY TO GOD...............................199
GOD CARES FOR THE CHILDREN........ 56
GOD IN HIS WORKS (Opening Service)...222
GOD IS IN HIS HOLY TEMPLE............. 23
GOD IS LOVE...................................... 69
God is Love, His Mercy Brightens............ 64
GOD IS NEAR THEE........................107
GOD OF MY LIFE 26
GOD OUR HELP..................................115
GOD'S ALL EMBRACING LOVE 62
GOD'S CONSTANT CARE..................... 60
God Sends the Sunshine and the Rain......... 20
GOD'S LOVE FOR ZION... 66
GOD THE FATHER (Opening Service).....225
Go forth to the Harvest Field 149
Go Labor On; Speed and be Spent............150
GO ON!..124
Go Through the Gates, Prepare Ye the Way...143
Go to the Fountain and Drink..... 32
GO WORK TO-DAY.............................149
Great God! Let All our Tuneful Power 73
Great God of Nations now to Thee.. 210
Great God! to Thee my Evening Song 18
GREENVILLE..................................... 39

Hail! Source of Light of Life and Love........ 27
Hail the God of our Salvation.................. 63
Hail to the Lord's Anointed 189
HAPPY HOME..................................177
Hark, Hark, My Soul! Angelic Songs are Swelling.....................................126
Hark! Hark! with Harps of Gold..............190
Hark, My Soul! it is the Lord................165
Hark! the Sabbath Bells are Pealing 2
HARK? WHAT DESPAIRING CRIES 217

INDEX.

Hark! What mean those Holy Voices?......108
HARWELL......198
Hath thine heart grown very weary?......133
Hear the pleading of the Son......183
HEAR THE PRECIOUS WORDS OF LIFE...166
HEAVEN IS OUR HOME......180
HE IS MY ROCK......111
HELP US TO PRAISE......4
Help to bear each other's burdens......163
HOLY SPIRIT, TRUTH DIVINE......48
How firm a foundation, ye saints of the Lord..117
How pleasant, how divinely fair......17
HOW SWEET TO THINK......206
How we miss our baby darling......204

If thy path is like night......111
If we only sought to brighten......162
I'LL REMEMBER MY CREATOR......19
I love the bright Spring-time......202
I LOVE THE GIVER MORE......25
I LOVE THY CHURCH......184
I love to see the beauteous flowers......25
I'm out on an ocean......86
IMMANUEL SHALL COME TO THEE......135
Immortal love forever full......98
In the cross of Christ I glory......102
Into the light of God's glorious love......156
I read the dear old promise......59
I sing the mighty power of God......71
I think when I read that sweet story of old...76
I want to be more like Jesus......92
I WILL LIFT UP MINE EYES......51
I will not go doubting......112
I will rejoice with gladness deep......119

Jehovah God! thy gracious power......123
JESUS AND THE CHILDREN......74
JESUS MAKE ME HOLY......83
Jesus needs the little children......159
JESUS SHALL REIGN......192
JESUS SPEAKS THE WORD......75
Jesus took the little children......74
Joyful hearts and smiling faces......21
JOY IN BELIEVING......87
Joy! Joy! O hear the sound......196
JOY TO THE WORLD......81

KEEP ME EVER AT THY SIDE......40

LEAD KINDLY LIGHT......29
LEAD THOU ME......47
LEAD US GENTLY......42
Leave God to order all thy ways......116
LENOX......67
Let every mortal ear attend......173
Let us never complain......130
Let us sing of Jesus' love......97
Life has more of cheerfulness......40
LIGHT FROM THE HEIGHTS BEYOND...137
LIGHT FROM THE OTHER SHORE......110
List to the song......69
LITTLE PANSY......212
LONGING FOR CHRIST......103
Look ye saints......201
LORD AND MASTER OF US ALL......98
Lord God of Holiness......10
Lord, my heart is rested, strengthened......40
Lord! I desire with Thee to dwell......103
LOVE DIVINE......82
Love is the strongest tie......186

MARCHING AT THE KING'S COMMAND...154
Marching, marching, marching on the way...154

MARLOW......27
MIGHTY TO SAVE......113
MISSIONARY HYMN......189
MORE LABOR FOR THE LORD......146
MORE LIKE JESUS......92
MORNING HYMN......22
MORNINGTON......171
My Country 'tis of Thee......2 b
MY ETERNAL HOME......179
My God, how endless is thy love......60
My God, thy boundless love I praise......68

NEARER I'D BE......36
Nearer my God to thee......34
NEARER THE CROSS......84
NEARER TO THEE......80
Nearer to thee is my prayer, O Savior......80
Nearer to thy heart of love......36
NETTLETON......11
NEVER COMPLAIN......130
No more delaying, God's call obeying......133
Not long ago the moon was dark......219
Now all the bells are ringing......200

O Christ, our Master, we would sow......161
O city of the Lord......188
O come, O come, Immanuel......135
O COULD I SPEAK......86
O Father dear, I know, I feel......9
O Father, hear my pleading prayer......30
O, for a shout of joy......67
O GENTLE SHEPHERD......78
O harken to your Savior, Friend......166
Oh, beautiful beautiful flowers......213
Oh, for a thousand tongues to sing......100
Oh, pray on, my brother, and toil to the end...44
Oh, render thanks to God above......8
Oh, still in accents sweet and strong......146
Oh! that I were pure in heart......43
OLD HUNDRED......7
O listen to the story sweet......168
O, love! O, life! our faith and sight......91
O my Father, thee I thank......22
ON THE JERICHO ROAD......158
ON TO THE FIELD......149
ONWARD, DAY BY DAY......141
ON WHAT ARE YOU BUILDING?......114
ORTONVILLE......120
O Savior, come and walk with me......37
O turn toward Zion......138
OUR COUNTRY'S BANNER......208
Our Father gave the life we own......5
OUR FATHER IS TRUE......112
Our God, our help in ages past......115
OUR TREASURES......205
OUT OF THE DEPTHS......30
OVER LIFE'S WONDERFUL TIDE......86

Pansy, dearest little Pansy......212
Passing through the lowly valley......137
PETERBOROUGH......173
POOR SINNER, LOV'ST THOU ME?......165
PORTUGUESE HYMN......117
POWER, WISDOM AND GOODNESS......71
PRAISE THE LORD......21
Praise the Lord, we now are free!......145
Praise the Lord, ye heavens adore him......21
PRAISE TO GOD (Opening Service)......224
PRAISE TO THEE......15
PRAYER FOR FORGIVENESS......53
PRAYER FOR PURITY......43
PRAY ON, MY BROTHER......44

INDEX.

Press On! Press on a Glorious Throng......133
Press On! Press On! Ye Sons of Light........151
PRESS ON TO WIN THE PRIZE 133
PUBLIC WORSHIP.................. 17

RALLYING SONG 215
RESURRECTION 203
Return, O wanderer, now return..............174
RING THE TEMPERANCE BELLS........214
ROLL ON THE TIDINGS................187
ROWING AGAINST THE TIDE............128

SABBATH HOME..... 12
SABBATH MORNING 6
Sadly Bend the Flowers......................109
SAILING OVER LIFE'S WONDFRFUL
  TIDE...........:............................. 86
SAVIOR, BE EVER NEAR 45
Savior, Bless a Little Child 52
SAVIOR, BLESS THE LITTLE ONES..... 52
SAVIOR, WALK WITH ME 37
See Israel's Gentle Shepherd Stand............. 90
SERVANTS OF CHRIST, ARISE 148
Shall We All Meet at Home in the Morning?..175
SING HIS PRAISES 5
SING OF JESUS.............................101
SING OF JESUS' LOVE 97
Sometimes a Light Surprises 87
Soon May the Last Glad Song Arise 194
Source of Life Beyond my Vision............. 31
SOWING FOR THE HARVEST..............161
SOWING THE SEED OF THE KINGDOM...147
Speak Kindly, Speak Kindly to Young and to
  Old..155
Stand Up! Stand Up for Jesus..................139
STOCKWELL 63
STRENGTH AND GUIDE 116
STRONG SON OF GOD 93
Sweet Are the Promises.....................121
SWEET BELLS OF LOVE..................... 20
SWEET HOUR OF PRAYER 53
SWEET IS THE WORK, MY GOD, MY KING 3
SWEET IS THY MERCY, LORD 49

TELL ME OF HEAVEN.....................176
TEMPERANCE (Opening Service)............233
TEMPERANCE BATTLE CALL............216
Teach Us to Feel as Jesus Prayed 94
THANKSGIVING HYMN 10
THAT SWEET STORY OF OLD............... 76
THAT THEY MAY BE ONE.................183
THE ANGELS' SONG........................196
The Christian Warrior, See Him Stand 152
The Day of Resurrection....................203
THE GLORIOUS LIGHT....................131
THE GLORIOUS WORLD ON HIGH........181
The God of Wisdom, God of Love 104
The Golden Glow is Paling 218
The light is shining on the way..............131
THE LOVE OF GOD......................... 65
The Lord is Our Shepherd, our Guardian and
  Guide.....................................118
THE LORD IS ARISEN 202
THE MASTER'S MESSAGE 88
The Morning Light is Breaking...............190
THE PURE IN HEART.... 106
There is a Home, a Happy Home ... .177
There is a Land of Pure Delight 178
There is a little lonely fold 78
There is a light, a shining light...............125

There is a glorious world on high............181
There is a world we have not seen..... ..181
There's a Message from Jesus to thee 88
There's a Voice Comes to my Soul 75
There's a Voice I hear, and it Calls me Near...164
There's a Wideness in God's Mercy......... 65
THERE'S LIGHT ABOVE THE CLOUDS....142
THE SABBATH BELLS..................... 2
THE SHINING LIGHT.....................125
THE SPIRIT AND THE BRIDE SAY, COME.170
The Spirit in Our Hearts....................171
THE STARS...............................218
THE TRUE AND ONLY LIGHT............218
THE TRUMPET'S CALL OBEY............153
THE UNIVERSAL SONG...................188
THE WANDERER'S WELCOME............168
THE WAY, THE TRUTH, THE LIFE....... 89
The Wrong that Pains my Soul Below........122
This is Not my Place of Resting... 179
This is our Country's Celebration...........208
THOU ART MY SHEPHERD 70
Thou Art, O God, the Life and Light........ 72
Thou Art the Way—to Thee Alone 89
Thou Grace Divine, Encircling All........... 62
THY BOUNDLESS LOVE I PRAISE........ 68
THY KINGDOM COME..................... 35
Thy Way, Not Mine, O Lord................105
'TIS A STORY FULL OF WONDER........195
'Tis Easy to Glide With the Ripples..........128
TO-DAY THE SAVIOR CALLS.............169

UNBOUNDED LOVE..................... ... 73
UNDER THE SHADOW OF THY WING....119
UNFAILING LOVE.......................... 59
UNTIL WE MEET AGAIN 221
UPWARD.................................. 38
Upward Father, turn our Eyes................ 38

WAIT AND TRUST.........................109
We are but Little Children.................... 77
We are but Strangers here...................180
WEBB.....................................139
WE DO IT UNTO THEE....................114
We Give Thee but Thine Own...............144
We gladly come to the House of God....... .. 12
WELCOME SACRED DAWN................ 13
WELCOME TO OUR SABBATH HOME..... 24
We Long to See that Happy Time.... 193
WE MAY NOT FORGET................... 14
WE SHALL SEE IT BY-AND-BY......... 204
WE SHOULD HEAR THE ANGELS SING-
  ING......................................162
WE SOON SHALL MEET ABOVE..........206
We wait in faith, in prayer we wait...........120
WE WILL LABOR 159
We're a Band of Happy Children............. 16
WE'RE CHILDREN OF A KING........... 16
What a friend we have in Jesus............... 96
When darkest storms your path surround....121
When faith is weak and joy has fled..........176
When the day of life is brightest............. 47
WHERE HE LEADS I'LL FOLLOW.........121
While Thee I seek protecting Power..........113
WHILE WE WORK FOR JESUS...........157
WHISPERINGS OF GOD'S LOVE........... 61
WILL YOU STAND UP FOR JESUS?......134
WHO CAN SPEAK SUCH WORDS?....... 79

Ye sons of earth, arise......... 172

Zion stands with hills surrounded............. 66

www.ingramcontent.com/pod-product-compliance
Lightning Source LLC
Chambersburg PA
CBHW032136160426
43197CB00008B/664